76 FEATHERS:

ALWAYS REMEMBERED.
A MOTHER'S JOURNEY THROUGH
LOSS, GRIEF & HOPE

Jeannine Brown Miller

Dedication

To my beloved son, Jonathan, who through the life he led and through his passing has provided me with learning to live life to its fullest, to live in the moment and to realize that faith provides us with all of our needs.

Dear Reader,

I am so glad you chose to read 76 Feathers!

For the first several years after the sudden death of my son, I spent many hours daily writing in my personal journal to include my feelings. It was healing, and it allowed me to reflect mindfully and to determine how I would put back the pieces of my shattered heart.

Through this reflective time, I have learned so much about my purpose in life. What I have come to through my own reflective thoughts and feedback from others is that I need to continue to help others. Many friends and acquaintances have asked me to help other mothers who are grieving. I have spent a great deal of time doing just that. As you can imagine, as we seek to help others, we are helped in return. I have met some of the best and strongest women out there as a result. Their strength is inspiring and we continue to keep one another "lifted" in spirit. We are there for one another and I am grateful to have such friends who came into my life as a result of a common lifelong journey of living without our children. This is a bond like no other.

My approach to writing this is to make it feel like I'm sitting with you personally, chatting about life and trials that make us who we are despite the gravity of the trial. In order to take you there, I describe my journey from the moment I lost my son to today. Some of it is very raw, but that's reality and it's necessary to express the depth of my loss. I then take you on a path that will help you with whatever you are finding oppressive and translate such suffering into how you can live your best life. We all have a purpose, and finding that is key. Mine, I have learned, is to help others any way I can and I do so through my professional work and living my best life through my personal struggles.

The beginning of the book carries you through the day I lost my son, the aftermath and the extent of how much we learned Jonathan impacted people's lives. To this day, we continue to hear stories, even by those who never met him.

The second part of the book includes messages from Heaven, signs and miracles if you will. Believe it: I didn't, until I experienced such miracles regularly. I then move on to testimonials from people, as that is most impactful to learn about how one young life can change and help others through the toughest moments, even if it is now from Heaven.

Through descriptions of Jonathan's life and who he was to others, the concept of "angel on Earth" kept coming to me in a variety of ways through many different people. I do believe in angels, perhaps Jonathan was heaven-sent. I truly believe that happens and have read a lot about that since I have been urged to see his life in the extraordinary way others have.

Finally, I focus on how I cope. Ideas on how others suffering could move toward handling such a tragic situation in a manner that is full of hope. Seeing the positive, helpful methods of dealing with grief, I pray, will help you.

So I now invite you to kick back, grab a cup of coffee and join me through this book as I describe my journey of trauma, grief, love, faith, and hope.

As my son left me with this message I share it with you "Live by Faith, One Day at a Time." It makes all the difference!

May God bless you with His unending gift of love, peace, and hope.

"Wow.. *Yes, the response to J's death was a unique experience in my life. Having been in this business for 22 years I have unfortunately dealt with this before. The response to J's death was unlike anything I have experienced. I have come to believe that his life, though short, was given to all of us by God for a specific reason. That sounds peculiar perhaps, but I have thought about this often and I truly believe that J was different. The way he loved all and all loved him. His desire to serve others, his ability to settle differences, bring people together. I know you often say that he had his faults and his teenage ways but when you look at the life of all saints, they were human, with all the faults and misgivings of their humanness. Yet they were outward, visible, tangible signs of the heavenly father, the son and the spirit. Putting his story, this story on paper would be extremely important. A seemingly ordinary life, yet in death so extraordinary. That is saintliness. That is Christ-like. I hope I am not overstepping my bounds with these words. If you recall I mentioned in my remarks the life of Padre Pio. An ordinary man, a simple hardworking priest. Yet through words, deeds, actions and his physical being he becomes a visible sign of the Father in our lives. To me that is Jonathan. I carry his picture in my wallet, next to my boys and will always. Not only because I do not want to forget him, but more importantly what his life has meant to me and how it allows me to be closer to my God. Again, I hope I have not upset you. I have always considered you and Kevin more than just one of my families. From our earliest meetings in 9/06 you always challenged me/us to be our best. To serve the* *individual needs of your son. At first I was taken aback by your approach. But unlike other parent encounters, I never felt attacked. You wanted our best at all times. You wanted us to think outside the box to create success for your son. That is what being a professional educator is all about. Our work with and for you, Kevin and Jonathan made us all better administrators, teachers, and professionals. Here again, his life is touching people in a unique way. "*

Paul (Paul J. Casseri – Principal, Lewiston Porter High School, now Superintendent of Lewiston Porter)

As you can see from the above letter to me, this is among so many others who wanted to hear about our journey. It inspired me to write this book now, ten years since J's passing. To this day, family, friends, and community members felt our story needed to be shared and have encouraged me to move forward. While we weren't sure how we would impact others just by sharing our coping, hearing from others how they are stronger when trials hit them inspired us to do the same. They felt the life and story of a young boy that had as much impact as J did should be told. Since my approach to coping is writing, it made it easy to get the content for this book and our journey. It started from my personal journaling.

This path has been nothing short of a miracle, as I never thought I could be in the place I am now after such a devastating loss. You will see the common theme of coping and healing is focused on a strong faith and relationship with God. I can't see walking this path without divine intervention, every step of the way. My life as a child was seemingly "perfect," without any stress to speak of and I had the "home court" advantage of a strong, loving family with parents that were, by all accounts, "perfect!" This foundation, I now know, was to prepare me for what was to come. Our life works that way. God maps out our journey before we are even born. God provides us with what we need all the way through. It is up to us to allow Him to guide us and all will be "well." The difficulties that I have encountered have been significant trials. I'm not saying I am that different from others. I'm just expressing that I had many obstacles that were extremely challenging. In fact, just about every type of significant life occurrence that usually "breaks" people has happened to us. The death of my son was just the tip of the iceberg.

Briefly allow me to share a bit about my journey prior to the death of Jonathan (J). I almost lost my first-born on two different occasions. Long before the loss of my boy, a fire destroyed our house and could have taken my first-born child's life, then just a baby. Eighteen years later, she was almost killed in a car accident, being hit head-on by a truck as she drove a small sedan.

We also had a brief period of financial difficulties. I was struggling in a job I had held for seventeen years, which created a desire to leave. Then, my son's death happened. I am like everyone else, with ongoing struggles in this life. The only good of each one is the profound role the love of family and friends has played, as well as the immeasurable love of God and the strength of faith.

Please allow me to take you through one family's, one person's journey through tragedy.

Here are some of the common mantras that guide my life.

Death is a completion, a graduation, a reward for a life well lived...

God promises a safe landing, not a calm passage.

I pray to accept exactly what I am given and walk this road without complaint...

Success is the value you give and determining and following the path to your purpose.

A tough journey requires recognizing your needs and tending to them to provide the strength needed to "carry the heavy crosses"...we all have the strength but like any challenge we need to "believe" we can do it!

Photo credit Scientific Magazine

Contents

Chapter 1

November 15, 2009

It was a typical Sunday. Jonathan, whom we call "J," was attending nine o'clock mass that morning alone, which he loved to do. It was funny that many people would notice how J was a regular, being a teenager, people do notice when young kids are at church - especially on their own. Afterward, Jonathan would meet us for breakfast. The focus of the conversation that morning was J's recent acceptance to Niagara University. Nothing was more important to him than that at this time, early in his senior year of high school. He loved Niagara and was so proud of his ability to go there. Being a student with his share of academic struggles, this was beyond gratifying and affirming of his abilities and future. After our breakfast, J went on to hang out with a few friends for a few hours before returning home for our family Sunday meal together.

After dinner, J mentioned that he was headed to Niagara to swim for a workout. He had recently finished football season and swimming helped relieve some aches and pains he had. Prior to going, he asked his sister, Lauren, if she would make him a cake and if he could borrow her goggles. Lauren agreed to both requests, and while she was finding her goggles for him to use, J went to the store for a cake mix to drop off prior to swimming. J came home, picked up his goggles, and off he went.

Shortly after J left the house, Lauren heard a crash-like sound, so she immediately called J to see if it was him. He answered the phone, and when she asked him if he was okay, he laughed.

"Yes I'm fine," he said, as he drove up the hill toward Niagara.

That would be the last conversation he would ever have.

Meanwhile, Kevin, his father, and I were visiting my parents, as we did almost daily- and Sundays for sure. While we were there, my mom indicated that she felt J's eyes weren't so good. J had taken her grocery shopping on Saturday, as he often did given her declining eyesight. She noticed that he would return with items that weren't exactly as she asked him to retrieve. I immediately mentioned that we'd get him in for a checkup ASAP, although we didn't notice anything like that ourselves. I called J's cell to talk to him about his eyes as we were discussing it, but there was no answer and no return call. I assumed he was doing his laps in the pool.

Kevin and I left my parents' home and began driving back to our house. On the way, we came upon emergency lights flashing and blocked roadways, specifically in front of the campus area of Niagara University, where J was headed to swim. My intuition put me in a panic, and I immediately asked Kevin to head into the campus toward the recreation center where the pool was and where J had been headed.

I was paralyzed with fear.

Kevin was trying to calm me down and saying that all was well, but I wasn't convinced of that. We arrived at the center and didn't see J's SUV. I asked Kevin to go and see if J checked into the center, and when I saw Kevin coming out, he looked a bit worried and indicated that J had not signed in.

"We have to get to the emergency site," I said.

He was trying to get me not to focus on that, but I insisted.

A mother's intuition had me absolutely convinced: this was our tragedy.

As we redirected toward the site, we came upon the police vehicles. They stopped us, saying they couldn't let us continue toward the site of the "accident." I insisted they tell me if a vehicle with the license plate "JMILL" was involved, at which point they were trying to get me to go back to our car. I pushed back and repeatedly asked them about the license plate, but they didn't reply.

I went back to our car and just sat in complete distress. Within a short time, two people came walking toward us. I jumped out of the car.

"Sit tight," I told Kevin. "This is going to be bad for us."

Our worst fear was confirmed.

I immediately asked if anyone else was involved, and when I found out that there wasn't, I knew it was just our heartache and grateful no one else was injured.

We learned through a witness that our J passed out while driving and his SUV veered into a tree. The witness happened to be an EMT and jumped out of his vehicle to try to help J. He quickly learned there was no heartbeat, and now with his SUV hitting the tree, his body was quite "broken" head to toe.

Given the tragic nature of this news and our numb, deep, overwhelming sadness, we were driven away by the ministers at the scene. Kevin went one way and I went another, as we split up to be sure we got to the key people that needed to know immediately. I asked to get me back to my parents' home. Kev needed to go tell Lauren and be with her. J's sister Alyssa was traveling abroad at this time so she learned shortly thereafter.

When I ran into my parents' home to deliver the news, I screamed.

"J is dead," I cried.

My dad literally flew backwards on the couch, crying.

"No, no, no this can't be!" my mom yelled.

Trying to console them was my immediate challenge, as I was worried about how this would affect them given their vulnerability due to their age – they were well into their mid-80s at that time. My brother Chris and his wife Sue came to my parents' house to be with us after they heard, too.

After a short time, I wanted to get to our Lauren to console her and wanted to just be home. As overwhelmed as Lauren was, she quickly recalled hearing that "crash" right after J left the house, but figured it was "just in her head".

Perhaps it was a premonition.

My parents joined me and stayed that night, as we all just couldn't let each other go. Not for one second.

Shortly after we were home, the word got out into our close-knit community. My entire family came over to be with us, and our pastor was called. We had to get to our youngest daughter, Alyssa, who was traveling to Amsterdam that very evening. In no way could we let her hear through social media or any other form. Lauren and my best friend made that call to Alyssa, and needless to say, her journey home had to begin. And what an overwhelming journey that was for her - she just received news that her baby brother was gone. News picked up the story, and being from a small community where we know most people, this became a community tragedy, we quickly learned. Our house was nonstop people in and out. Hundreds of students and others stopping by, and no one seemed to be consolable.

The cause of J's death is unknown, as he died while he was driving. They believe either a heart issue or head injury from football may have been to blame.

Either way, we are not to know why we lost our otherwise perfectly healthy teenage boy to a sudden, tragic death.

November 15, 2009 forever changed our lives.

Chapter 2

DOES GOD SEND ANGELS ON EARTH?

Honestly, as one can imagine, I spent all my days - minutes - actually thinking about every aspect of this profound loss. I was grateful that so many kept reaching out to share their stories about J and help to build us back up piece by piece. After all of what we learned from the hundreds of people who addressed us in so many ways, I began to wonder more and more about J. We all love our children and think the world of them I'm sure but this was different. Honestly, he was so much more than I ever imagined as described by so many others. I was overwhelmed by all the good he did for so many in just seventeen short years on this earth.

Contemplating how much impact such a young soul had, I began to question how he seemed to be able to be "everywhere," but yet with us at home so much as well. How did one young kid have such impact? On two different occasions, two of J's friends mentioned that J was "different," he was "better than the rest of us" in both similar messages with slight differences in expression.

Thinking about their sincere expressions of how he was so different, I actually asked myself: Could Jonathan have been an angel on earth?

You hear of angels among us, but did I have one in J? All that he did didn't seem possible given the structure and time of day he would have as such a young kid. School, work, home life, visits with family, sports, friends…how could he do so much? J was often described, particularly by some of the school personnel as having "Christ-like" characteristics. Our pastor at our church also felt he was "special" not knowing quite how to express what he meant. Those that are consistently described as "special," "not like us," J had an aura around him. He was "always to be at the right place at the right time to help others."

What is it about such people that make them stand out? The regular emails, Facebook messages and posts made me stop and ask: What is it that others see in him? And was J a "borrowed angel"?

Chapter 3

"VISIONARY" DREAMS OF JONATHAN

"It's not about death - it's about love and hope and loving connections that continue, even after death."(Bonnie McEneany- author of Messages from Loved Ones Lost on 9/11)

"Dreams of this nature are often heaven sent... reminding us of our loved one present to us... always...helping us through whatever "He" knows we need - to assist us through problems; to emphasize love is eternal; to protect us from a situation/harm; to help us find peace somehow with the loss"... Whispers of God's love by Mitch Finley

A friend contacted me once about a dream of Jonathan.

"I had a dream. J was really there. I could smell him, see him in full form, and we were actually hugging. Yes, I felt him."

The message from such dreams, which I learned were called "visionary dreams," was to "tell my mom I am fine and happy"…and so many did just that. Even though they prefaced with, "I hope I don't upset you but…"

Andrew, a cousin of J's, had a dream of our grandfather, who would be J's great-grandfather, with J and other relatives playing cards, smiling and waving to him. It was as if to show how content they were and, of course, happy to be together.

Steve, J's uncle and also his confirmation sponsor, had a special role in his life and took him on vacations with his son, also had a visionary dream. In the dream, Steve mentioned that he was working outside and heard a "hello," and it was J. J hugged him and Steve asked him why he hasn't contacted his parents. J showed his usual calm smile and was very content.

Richie, a dear cousin who had not seen J for over a year and regretted not seeing him now that he was gone, said that J came to him explaining to Richie that it was his time and he had to go but loved everyone and was very happy. Rich hugged him and could describe every piece of clothing on him.

Alyssa, one of J's sisters who, like mentioned, was away his last few months on Earth, particularly felt bad she had not seen him. J came to her in a similar manner to Richie, in that they hugged, they talked and spent time together, with all of us, having dinner together. J was only talking to her in this dream despite the rest of us being "there." He wanted her to let us know he is fine and "here" to take care of us so we understand that.

Jeff, Alyssa's husband and a dear friend of J's and like a big brother figure, had experiences he shared. Jeff and J were very much alike and spent a good deal of time together when he was over at our house. Jeff too described how real his dream was, they hugged and cried together. Jeff asked if he was in Heaven yet, the response, not yet...but I am happy and please let everyone know. When Jeff asked whether he would come to me since I have been so upset, J simply said..."no not now." Jeff was forever changed by this experience, as he was not sure of Heaven and God's role, but through this experience he received the gift of understanding that there is heaven and he now finds peace in that. Several years later, Jeff was in a near fatal accident. He needed to use a rental car due to his truck being totaled; the number of the truck was **"76,"** which was also J's football jersey number in high school. He realized right then just who protected him through this horrific accident.

Carmella, a distant cousin that remained close to my parents, had a dream different than those above, but the setting was that J's sisters, father and I were leaving church and behind Alyssa she vividly saw a white small figure following us out of church…when we entered the car, disappeared. She was so touched by this she had to call my mother to express her vision.

Andrea, another dear cousin who dreamt that it was actually before he died and the setting was such that it seemed to be his birthday and he came over to her house with some other people. He was happy as always, but somehow through this dream she was told that he would die and couldn't do anything to stop it. She wasn't as content after this dream as you can imagine, however the dream was a week after his funeral.

AS- a childhood friend of J shared this:

"I just wanted to say hello and share a touching dream I had about Jonathan. The other day I fell asleep on my couch and started dreaming about seeing a reunion with all my friends and Jonathan was the first person I saw. Immediately I gave him a huge hug and began crying in his arms, once I calmed myself down I asked him why I don't see him as much as I used to, and he answered saying in a lighthearted and happy manner that he always spoke in that I don't turn around enough. I've had countless dreams about him but in all of them he never spoke, this was the first time he ever said anything to me. I've been having a hard time with what happened and I truly believe that what he was trying to tell me is that I need to talk about him more instead of just holding in what happened. I believe He was trying to show me that he was happy and in a good place and was trying to help me through the pain. It was undoubtedly the most realistic and touching dream I have ever had in my entire life, I woke up in a pool of tears and just couldn't believe it, I felt so close to Jonathan and still felt his big arms around me hugging me. I really miss Jonathan more than anything and still feel the pain every day, but seeing him so happy and looking out for us all really helped to put some of it to ease. I hope all is well and would love to see you all during the summer. Tell everyone I say hello and send my love"

Another friend

CP, a high school friend of J wrote in a message to me…."J came to me in a dream last night. I've been suffering over my stupid ex-boyfriend for so long and knew J knew that. All night I was having these terrible dreams about my ex, and just before I woke up my final dream was with J-Mill. Someone beeped the horn outside and I didn't want to go outside because I was sad. I finally got up, opened the door and saw J pull in my driveway in the Corolla. I think one of his football teammates was in a car behind him. I started bawling and he got out and he gave me the biggest hug. Mrs. Miller, I thought my mom was trying to wake me up or my dogs were on me because the hug he gave me was so real. I could feel him! I was crying in his arms and J said "hey it's alright, if you need me I'm right here"…

Another cousin of Jonathan, wrote "I had a very vivid dream about J that I wanted to share with you. J, the cousins, and I were in Vermont at the lake house. For some reason, J would only be with us for a few more hours. We didn't know how long or what was happening to him. It was confusing and sad because we didn't understand where he was going. In the dream, we were keeping close to him as much as possible, knowing he only had a few more hours with us. J looked perfectly healthy, happy, and was running around, having the time of his life, without a care in the world, well knowing that he didn't have much time left with us. He was cherishing every moment, and kept laughing and running around, joyfully. I asked him what he wanted to do before he left us. He didn't answer my question, but kept laughing and smiling with an expression on his face that there was no need for anyone to worry about him. This was the first profound dream I had of J and it brought a lot of comfort to everything we were experiencing. The dream felt like it was J's response to our frustration regarding his death. It was an incredibility real and sincere experience to see him at peace."

Common themes

So, what were these messages all about? Why were they to be sure they told me? They were so "real" and "J was there and they hugged him, a dream like no others"…the dreams were described as something they never felt before, not like a regular dream. I have later learned that these are referred to as "visionary" dreams. Such dreams are when you can touch them, smell them and see the details of what they are wearing, feeling like they were "really there." The message was, I am happy, miss everyone, but happy and will be around all of us. A sense of peace and a description of the dream as "serene" was also a common theme. J was always described as being in a hurry to "go back"...anxious to be back in Heaven and on to his final "level" or "graduation," it seemed. He often didn't answer their questions but rather was there to provide messages only. He was often described as having that beautiful, peaceful smile we all will always remember, his genuine expressions providing such warmth and of course his well known hugs!

Encounters

Encounters shared by others are intended for us to truly believe in how those who leave this Earth, remain close to us, in a different form. Love never dies.

One day I received a call from one of J's classmates. He was upset, but he needed to share his encounter. He was driving and had an accident where he nearly died. He always kept a picture of J in his car as his guardian angel and sure enough, the picture was the first thing he saw when he realized he was okay.

Further, one of J's classmates had a memorial rubber wristband made and many people wore it for years - some still do. Some of them mentioned they keep it in their car as a comfort of J being with them.

Another classmate was in an accident as well. When the state trooper talked to him after the accident, he saw J's picture and the trooper, who also knew of J said to him, "your friend is watching over you. You could have died. Believe that." This person indicated that he definitely believes J is always with him.

A Facebook message that was touching and indicative of how J's friend's viewed him now:

> "Not many are lucky enough to have a guardian angel like you
>
> Lord I'm so thankful, please don't think I don't feel grateful, I do
>
> Just grant me the strength that I need, for one more day to get through
>
> So homie this is your song, I dedicate this to you
>
> I love you JMILL" RT

Writing blogs and on posts on Facebook became a regular part of my healing. I would share my thoughts and coping journey regularly. I have been asked to speak to groups and one-on-one with other parents who lost a child. It is good to be able to help others as you are helping yourself. But the one thing that has had an overwhelming impact is my sharing of interactions and messages from Heaven. I'll never forget talking to my dad about my experiences and he stated that miracles are meant to share, so in my writing I did so. People who never met him, but know me got to know him through my memorials that I have for J as well as the "messages" that he sends me that inspired them so much that they now connect him with some of their miracles experienced.

Chapter 4

A BORROWED ANGEL – WHY DID HE HAVE TO LEAVE SO SOON?

The question I ask daily. It's been ten years and that question remains. Actually, it gets even more frustrating when I realize how much of him growing we are missing and how much we miss him at each and every family milestone and event. He loved people so much, especially family. He was fun, loving, and compassionate. Why did he have to leave this Earth so soon?

When I began this journey I never thought I would come out of it a whole person again. I was a happy, strong, positive person by nature. November 15, 2009 changed this person. Changed this person in many ways. I described my situation as being "shattered," specifically having a "shattered heart."

What is apparent in every turn of my life is that it is only by the grace of God, the strength, peace and positive outlook I have in life that began to come back. This happened much quicker than I ever thought it would have. I really never expected to be okay, ever, because I just didn't know how I could pull myself back together. There were times early on that I didn't know if I could even laugh again, smile again, find joy again. I describe myself as fine crystal that shattered that was slowly put back together, but never to be exactly the same because all of the pieces are no longer there. And so I realized that not being exactly the same person is fine, in fact, a better version of me is the result.

We really don't know our strength, or the level of our faith we possess, unless we are challenged, tested or with this loss, bulldozed. J was my baby, my only boy and one of the extraordinary joys of my life. I am fortunate to say that each of my kids is extraordinary in their own way. God blessed me abundantly and despite Him taking J back too soon, the gift of J's life is what I focus on. Oh, how lucky I was to be able to raise this amazing boy.

So when I ask myself this question, why did he have to leave so soon, I realize that his mission was complete despite his short time on earth, and it was now up to us to be sure we live our life as intended by

God so we can fulfill our own mission in life. That's a tall order, but with God, everything is possible.

Was J a "borrowed angel"? Honestly, I can't believe I'm even contemplating this, but I guess I am intended to and reflect on what this all means.

This title here is taken from a song called "Borrowed Angels" by Kristin Chenoweth. This song was sent to me by one of J's classmates who felt the lyrics described J's life. We learn that those who are dying see beyond this world as they are completing their long-awaited journey to Heaven.

An experience comes to mind here. My grandfather was dying in a hospital bed, and it was a very sad time. My mother or one of the family members would always be by his side. One night, as my mother sat beside him, my grandfather said to her, "I see an angel Ro, a baby boy." At this time, no one but my husband and I knew that I was pregnant. When my mother mentioned this to me, I immediately began to cry and told her about a new life to come. We didn't know by any means that it was a boy. It wasn't until June 25, 1992 that we learned that he was in fact the "angel, baby boy" "seen" by my grandfather who was born and we named him Jonathan Harold.

The news of this new baby was a pleasant surprise. Jonathan, (later to be called J-Mill by his friends) was a beautiful gift from God, our only son and the youngest of three beautiful children. His sisters lovingly embraced him and helped take care of him even though they were only four and two years older than he. And so this beautiful life began.

The birth of J brought about many changes to us as a family. We suddenly needed to move and purchase a larger home, a larger vehicle and of course, baby things appropriate for boys. So many exciting changes and life seemed so perfect.

J was always a focus of the family, most of all because he drew the attention. He had a nature of being so lively, curious, and always into things. J walked at nine months old and was advanced in many activities. He had his struggles, most of which related to fine motor skills and some other activities. J was so much fun, so loved and such a joy to have among us. He always lit up a room with his warm smile and obvious appreciation and love for everyone he encountered.

In the early years, J brought his loving spirit to those that assisted us in caring for our children as we both worked full time. To this day, those who watched him express their love for him and the happiness he brought them as a young child. He was a challenge no doubt, and strong-willed. He didn't care much about school work, drawing, coloring, puzzles or "quiet" activities but rather, cowboys, robbers, policeman, firefighter, hockey, football, basketball, rollerblading, running, playing and always wanting to be with his cousins and other buddies. That never changed throughout his life and oh how we learned the love he had for his "buddies" and strangers alike!

J loved school, not because he loved the work or enjoyed the challenges of academics, but he loved school because he was among other kids that he began to love early on. Actually, school brought challenges that turned out to be lifelong struggles. He had struggles that he turned into successes despite the difficulties related. J had a rare learning disability that was extremely hard to detect especially since by all accounts, he appeared to be very bright making the struggles hard to spot until he was older. The disabilities affected his vision, coordination, fine motor skills, and other physical issues that resulted in difficulties with writing, drawing and extensive math problems. J had physical limitations that weren't obvious, but caused him to struggle with athletics that he loved so much. Running was a huge challenge for him despite his outward strong, physical, healthy appearance. That didn't stop him either. He played every sport including, hockey, baseball, basketball, soccer, karate, and football. Never a star for his athletic ability, but as we now have learned he was a star for his spirit, his character, his love for his teammates, the camaraderie that being part of a sports team brings. In fact, so much so, that to this day, the football coaches of Lewiston Porter High School give an award to a senior who embodied the character and spirit of "J Mill".

What amazed me as his mother is the perseverance that he had despite his shortcomings. God gave him the ability to handle struggles with so much grace and humor that he made others comfortable with their issues as well. He never let anyone or any obstacle get him down. He was blessed with the ability to look at life through rose-colored glasses and the glass was ALWAYS more than half-full! God blessed him with gifts and grace to persevere and show us all how obstacles are just that, they do not define who we are nor the impact we can have. How J handled his struggles was to be an inspiration to others and contributed to defining his "purpose" in this life. This young boy of mine has transferred this to me in a powerful way.

To know J was to love him, his warm smile, his big gentleness. He was a "gentle giant." He was one who wanted to make others happy and would do so in a quiet way.

Chapter 5

A sudden, unexpected death of my child, acceptance of God's plan

The first night was like a living nightmare. I literally kept looking outside thinking that this didn't really happen and he will be home soon. I kept grabbing my phone, thinking, he will call and it will be okay. My husband and I just held each other night after night. Crying until passing out, waking up just to relive this nightmare day after day.

I have met with many other mothers having lost a child and by and large there are many feelings that are the same. It is the way we choose to handle this extreme pain that makes or breaks us all.

How do I begin to describe how I felt? Let's begin with saying numb, physically sick, emotionally torn apart, sobbing from your toes, empty, lost. It's like you are falling down a cliff with no end in sight, fearful, confused. The first few days were agonizing. Twenty-four hours were eternity and getting through any given day, feeling somewhat impossible at times. It was "one moment at a time" that was about all I could handle. Prayer, constant prayer, asking for strength, asking for the "why" which was never to come, asking for the ability to function and be able to smile again was my constant request to God.

Then that feeling of wishing the pain would go, such an extraordinary pain, even if it meant not to awake each day. Yes I did say that, living another day seemed too hard, that's how difficult this is. I lost sight of the good that remained around me in those early days and anything that would remove this unbearable pain was the goal. Shortsighted, I quickly realized but I had to admit, this was that hard.

The day I released J

The heavy heart was one of those physical effects that makes moving through a day even more difficult. It wasn't until one day I woke up and said to God: "God I accept that you needed J. I know you know best, but help me because I miss him and need him here as well. I want to believe this was for the greater good and God, please direct me so that my suffering turns into something for the good of others". It was almost as if at the moment I ended the prayer that intense heaviness lifted. For the first time in a month,

I actually felt the oppressive physical heaviness lift. God began His "magic" rather promptly. I was feeling peace once again, not without extreme sadness. There will never be a time that I don't miss J and that I don't think about him and long for him with me. But I do know that God knows best and I am committed to making the best out of my life, despite this difficult path now carved out.

What I learned, as I should have known, is that God gives us what we need. I wasn't listening. God gave me all I needed once I was open to receiving His unending gifts. The pain and suffering do get more bearable as you "practice" living with them. I pushed along despite how I felt. Gratefully, my nature is to look at the positives, the good in life, and so over a relatively short period of time I realized I had far too many reasons to keep moving forward, to show that it is possible to get through this and that I can rebound at some point, by the grace of God. I also had the drive of ensuring that my parents, husband and daughters needed to know, that I could rally and their lives mattered more than the suffering I felt in J's dying.

I turned another corner.

Within a few months, I was indeed back to a stronger, functioning, somewhat more peaceful version of me. I needed to get my life back in any way I could so I didn't fall into the dark path that this could take you on. So I began working three weeks after J's passing.

My work is a "place" I can get away and focus on problem-solving and coaching others, which was healthier than focusing on my pain and suffering. I love my profession, I enjoy my clients, and I have a passion for making things better for others, the heart of my consulting role. Thankfully, I have learned of my strong will to surpass struggles, to turn things around, because my love for life forces me to move away from sadness. It is too unnatural for me to be sad, actually for me it is exhausting. I also know that I have far too many reasons to be grateful, even if just for J's short life. What an amazing boy I was given to raise! How wonderful that I had him, if even for a short time! As they say, "it's better to have loved and lost, than not to have loved at all". So true. I have an amazing husband, and I still had my parents who were rapidly aging but still very much "there." My beautiful daughters, and now two new "sons," need I say more! I am amply blessed and I know it.

Coping

This book is a result of my coping. I use writing and reflection to cope. I wrote from my heart. I wrote from what I have learned from this horrific life experience. I wrote to reach others who are suffering to show that you can go on and be the best person possible, once again…maybe even a better person.

I read many, many books that helped me process the pain. So many were extremely helpful, so many touched on exactly how I felt right down to the words I used to describe my journey.

The bottom line is that for us, there was only one way to deal with this and that was to forge ahead. Our loss has to be made good, somehow, someway.

A extreme numbness comes over you when trying to comprehend the deep loss of a child. The numbness is a way to soften the deep sorrow and to allow you to focus on other things in life…the good in life…your work…the people here on earth with you that need you and need you to focus on them as well!

A hard role for me as a mother is first, trying to be strong and dealing with the depth of this pain, for the sake of others. It takes every ounce of my being to get up and go with that smile that everyone is so used to. I have learned that all eyes tend to be mostly on the mom's coping. The pressure is strongly felt.

I believe that God mends a broken heart if you "give him all the pieces". Holding on to them yourself and unable to put them together results in extreme loneliness and anger. I couldn't do that. It is against my nature to be angry and negative. I knew that God would help me through this. Just knowing myself that I could do this, provided the positive energy to move through.

There have been many, many songs that have reminded me of how happy J is in heaven. What God has planned for us when we meet Him in Heaven is beyond any joy we experience here. A dear friend of mine, who lost her seventeen-year=old son four years before J died, reminds me of this regularly. At times when I say that J would want to be here for certain events, she will remind me "there is no better event planner than God," centering my selfish desire to have J back here again. I feel that when I see J again and he greets me in Heaven, he will be smiling, singing, playing cards and just plain having fun…the best part of Heaven for J is that he was so easygoing that earthly life is a struggle that God determined was not where J should be, he need not struggle any longer. Despite his positive outlook related to his challenges, God knew that he did what he was to do and that it was time for eternal bliss.

There are clearly stages of grieving that we are all pretty much aware of. When we reach each phase and whether we move beyond them and then revisit them varies by person. At times you can feel that peace that you so long for. That feeling that you hope you can have more often than not. Just as easy, you may literally have one small thing that is either said or done that can trigger what turns into deep sorrow and sadness within minutes. There are medicinal purposes for crying and I have learned to go with it as often and cry as hard as necessary.

Accepting God's purpose for deciding it was Jonathan's time to leave this earth is the tough one. At times I really get it and understand that he more than fulfilled his purpose and changed lives for the better in just seventeen short years! As a mother of this child, that makes me so proud. After all, what else would I want from my children? Be good, be loving to all, help, and serve others. He did all that and so effectively. But why didn't God believe that he should be around to do even more?

Why would allowing so many of us suffer with losing J be so important in the big picture? We may never know this but we have to learn to accept that which we cannot change. The powerless nature of this type of loss is overwhelming. When you are the type of person that fixes things for everyone, this one becomes one of those situations that teaches you that the only "fix" for this one is to show strength and faith to others. That is my life journey.

So many people look to the closest members of the family when there is a deep loss to see how they will cope. As a family, we decided to try to be strong. To live as we always did as best we could. To make good of a life well lived that was full of love and happiness. To do otherwise would be a disservice to honoring J's life.

Reading and writing is my best therapy. I enjoy taking my heart and mind in different places by engaging in a good inspirational book. I'm hoping this serves as such for those of you reading it. Work also has helped me get through what can be very long days. Coping is exhausting!

I worried early on that I wouldn't be the person I was previous to losing Jonathan. My role in work and personal life is to solve problems, be there for others, be positive, be happy…but how would do I be able to do this? That was my "full-time job" the first few months after his death. I had to determine how I could turn my deep sadness into something that becomes more positive.

So many people have asked me how I am doing this. How much I am inspiring them by just coping and exerting positive comments and energy. This is one reason it was important to write this book. If I can help so many through such things as Facebook and my work, then maybe a book putting it all together could really give hope to those that experience significant challenges. Since I so enjoy reading books that offer some perspectives that help me, I thought it was important I do the same!

Accepting his death is a tricky one. One day as I woke up beginning my "discussion with God," I finally said, "God, I accept you wanting J back…please help me do something good given this tremendous loss I have to endure for the rest of my life." The physical relief of this level of acceptance was important as I mentioned in detail above. I felt so much better physically, taking such oppression and heaviness off my heart. The shattering of the heart remains, but the heaviness has lightened. I equate this feeling to Jesus carrying the cross on His knees. That visual never had the effect it has now. I actually look at that picture now and see myself in His place, and I realize that's the point of it. Dragging this cross I have been given, on my knees. Acceptance has allowed me to "stand" as I carry this cross now and move forward with strength and some peace. The cross is still "heavy" but the ability to carry it more easily comes with strength over time.

Although I will never agree with God's decision, I do accept it. I know He knows best. I believe that. I also know that my son is in a great place, a place he desires, a place of complete peace and tranquility. That's what he was all about. This Earth creates turmoil that, frankly, was against who J was as a person. God spared him existence in this life and rewarded him with welcoming him to Heaven before life could kill his beautiful spirit.

Death is not a negative "event" to me any longer. I see death as a completion, a reward for a job well done. Most of us take a lot longer to prove our worthiness to enter the gates of Heaven, if we get there at all. So when God does decide to choose to take someone, especially a young person, we know He wants them to do something even more, but now from the Heavens!

That we cannot see, touch, hear or smell makes us believe it doesn't exist. But with faith, we know there is existence beyond what we can literally experience. That's what gets us through. We know that J is in Heaven. We know that as a result of the visionary dreams but also because as his mother, I feel peace. I know he is forever happy, healthy and safe. What else can I ask for? Yes, I will forever miss him but I no longer have to worry that his life won't be great because it was and far more than I realized!

At times you seek ways to make things "feel" better. What can be good about no longer seeing your child be able to grow to an adult who had tremendous aspirations and all signals indicating he would be very successful? One thing that stands out is that we no longer have to worry about him. That is a big deal for any parent. Knowing your child loved life, was loved by so many and now the ultimate reward with no significant disappointments in his life. Who would want anything else for their child? We know though, that is generally not the case for all of us if we live long enough. Challenges are guaranteed. Disappointments, certainly but for Jonathan, those were minor and few and far between. He was a chosen one for sure. He had an unusual life of fun and happiness. What else would I have wanted for him?

Life is how we choose to perceive it!

I choose to look at what is rather than what is not. I feel strongly that we are in control of how we are going to handle any challenges and situations. It is up to us as to how we choose to perceive a situation. We may not have control over our life, but we have some significant control over how we handle the life God gives us. Knowing that God is giving us what we need to be our best, we confidently move forward.

Furthermore, if I don't live the life God has planned for me, I won't see my son again. My goal, of course, is to end up with J for eternity when my time comes. That would be Heaven and I have work to do to get there!

Chapter 6

THE CHALLENGE OF
HOW DO I LIVE FULLY

Not only did I feel I wouldn't be able to breathe or carry on without J, I really didn't know if I even had the stamina to try. I spend a lot of time reflecting and self-healing. I also do a great deal of this through many aspects of my work with people. My purpose in life is to be there for others, not to need others to be there for me. Well, this sure turned things around…at least temporarily, in a big way. I really didn't know what I would do. How would I ever be strong enough to be there for everyone else again? Oh God, I prayed, please help me. This is not only my livelihood but I don't know how to be the one that is in need. Help me to seek help. Help me so I can breathe and move each day, one minute at a time was all I could ask for in the first few weeks.

I began to pray differently. I used to be a prayer warrior, novenas almost nightly, the rosary, throughout the day, and before each meeting. Then all of a sudden I couldn't pray this way anymore. I no longer found comfort in evening prayers before going to sleep. Most of the time I fell asleep or passed out since I would cry so hard throughout the day that I was exhausted. The body is physically, spiritually, and emotionally in extreme turmoil.

I was not ever in a state that I would call depressed, however, I was very sad all the time. My heart was so heavy. Facing the demands and demons in life are something I do head on and quickly. I heal best when I face the hardest situations and work through them. I handled this no differently. I knew that my life was forever changed, I was given a challenge that was extreme and difficult however, I knew always, that God gives me what I can handle and I had to be up for the challenge. Not only be up for it, but find the good in it, as strange as that sounds. Focus on the blessings in my life and find a new way to be joyful and peaceful, the challenge of all challenges.

All I ever wanted of my kids was to be kind and loving to all. He mastered that. All I wanted was for my kids to be happy and healthy, J experienced all of that. Although I am challenged to live my life without him here on Earth, my faith guarantees that he is with me more now than ever. I have to find peace in that. One day I awoke to feel somewhat vibrant and ready for a new day. My heart although aching, wasn't as heavy.

I actually felt a warmth around me and peace that I used to know. How could this be, and so soon?

My parents who have recently both reunited with those in Heaven who went before them were always my rocks. They are the people that helped me understand those things in life that are often mysteries. It was my mother who told me that my deep faith is what is working through me now. I know God and feel His presence. My dad would say, the way I am living is "living a prayer" as he reflected on the good that I do for others, particularly the charity work I always love to do. My father also said that showing that I can cope with this challenge is also "living a prayer". It is through all of that that you are given the graces through God that you need to move on. My father reminded me that prayer comes in many forms, the most important being the life you live. I didn't realize this and I began to see once again, my God giving me the peace I need to continue my work and mission in life, once again, I am able to help others. That is the role I am most comfortable in.

Healing is a process

The process of healing is long and hard, but I had extraordinary situations in my life that are making this easier and coming sooner. I had no regrets with the life and the incredible relationship I had with my son. We enjoyed our times together always. He died as he lived: happy and healthy, so we don't have regrets on how he died, just that he died. He had a stellar reputation and was described by a newscaster as "wildly" popular. By that really, it is his character and loving of all was widely seen through his death. J accomplished what he wanted to. He had great plans for his future, but he was so happy with where his life was to date. Academics didn't come easy. Sports didn't come easy. But loving people and being kind did and that's his legacy!

Coming from a strong family who are all faithful people helps considerably. My two girls are mature beyond their ages. They have been my rock as well. When I was weak, they reminded me of God's role and the love He has for us. My husband has a similar nature to our son. He is kind, patient and loving. That goes a long way through good and bad times. We all seem to be dealing in a similar manner. God has given us all the peace to carry on. We can smile even though our hearts are aching. We can show others that life can go on even in the midst of the sadness we are experiencing. This is God's work and expectations of all of us and He is giving us what it takes to show others that faith and the deep love of our God is all it takes to move through any tragedy.

We live in a community that consistently shows us their love and support. There is simply no other better "prescription" to healing than being surrounding by love and prayer.

Chapter 7

REBUILDING THE FOUNDATION

I describe this challenge as a crumbling of our "foundation."

The pain and heaviness in my heart was so severe that I felt like I might die and at times, hoped I would, actually.

Can you believe I am saying that? Well, it is true.

Thankfully, that was just a few weeks after J's sudden death. My foundation was so strong and I know that has made "rebuilding" a bit easier. I moved through certain levels of grieving quite quickly due to the great life J led and our relationship being so strong and positive. There was no guilt, no what if's, no I should have's, no anger or fighting - just a beautiful, loving relationship with my dear son who was becoming a man, right before my eyes. He was so logical, so supportive, so always there to give you a smile or positive word to keep life joyful. He would help me with my business, always so proud of my work and the success of it.

Anger is there but only every now and then. I think there will always be some level of anger that he is gone, but it passes as I know God had a reason and I am abundantly clear, that J lived his mission to its fullest. I truly believe God takes us when our work on earth is complete. We are then rewarded with the gift of eternal life.

Prolonged sadness was not an option for me. Although I fully understand that this is common for many people, for me, such an emotion is wasted energy. Rather than falling into that, which is easy to do when you are faced with this type of challenge, I chose to put that energy to action, hence my writing, which is now this book.

We certainly spent some time in shock, as there is no other way your brain can process the extreme of such an unexpected sudden loss. At times, that shock, I believe, turns into a numbness, which is to me, a more conscious approach to balancing your sadness with how you must move on and function in your life.

Although there are times of extreme sadness and sobbing, the periods of time are much shorter, despite their intensity. More of my days are calmer, peaceful and there is laughing once again. I always loved to entertain and thought early on that desire would stop. But after four months, my want to have others over returned and I had the energy to fully entertain once again. My son always loved when I did so, and that made it more of a desire to return to some normalcy and happy times which was also a part of him through me living on.

Milestones to healing are something I celebrate to remind myself that I can do it. I don't focus on the fact that our son died, but rather that he lived. Therefore, celebrations must continue! We do so diligently as his birthday and anniversary of his passing on to eternal life come each year. They are our "official" days off of work. No real plans, no consistent events, we just make sure this time is to just "be" in honor of J.

Life-changing in so many ways

Every challenge changes us in some manner. Making extreme sadness into something positive is the real challenge. But I am able to do this, and I am in awe of this ability and often tried to understand how I was able to keep moving forward. I know my son has to have a role, and I know he is with me. How else could I do this? I have more days than not of complete peace and hope.

We will never know why God gave us this challenge and heavy cross, but we know we have it and we know we have to "carry the cross" high, to show our love for God, our faith through showing our strength to carry on. This we have learned, helps others and that is what God's challenge is for us. To live a life in such a way that others will come to know Him.

The life of a great person who had tremendous impact on each and every person he encountered isn't something that can be told about all of us. When such a person leaves this world so soon, we begin to doubt our faith, God's plans and reasons, our world around us, losing our sense of stability and security. If this person is close to you, you lose a significant part of you; the loss redefines you and your new life. With the tears comes anger, longing, sadness like nothing ever felt before and a future that seems uncertain and swiped right from under you…in a matter of seconds your life changes forever.

We may never get the answer to the question of why he had to leave us so soon, so suddenly and when his life was so full of happiness, success and a future full of promise. The most confusing part of this is how J left this earth, the circumstances still clouded with uncertainty, but process of elimination points to a heart ailment that no medical exam can detect or confirm. A tragedy it was, resulting in his SUV going into a tree further adding to the dramatic nature of this ending for those who don't understand why this happened. No cell phone use, no fooling around, no drinking, no speeding, no iPod or other distractions – typical causes of accidents.

So how do I make sense out of this?

What I've learned is that J's death was not an accident; it was an ending that God had planned for him as he lived his life – full and happy to the end without pain or suffering. Such pain and suffering is the challenge left for us.

J didn't experience the hitting of the tree – he was already experiencing the beauty of Heaven and the angels greeting him before his physical body was "broken" by the hitting of a tree while on his way to work out at the university he was to attend in the fall of 2010. Some would say that the "accident" was to bring attention to a beautiful life, a beautiful kid who touched more lives than anyone could have imagined - more than J imagined I am sure.

The news stations, the newspapers in all of Western New York and the coverage of the vigils and memorials were amazing. Hundreds of people attended his wake and funeral. Hundreds of cards and letters from individuals who J touched came to us. Such expressions continue on special days in memory of J. It is almost 10 years ago now (2019). How proud we are of the life J led.

When we complete our mission in life, God takes us back. It was clear after learning of the impact of our dear son, that he had completed his mission in seventeen short years. We couldn't have asked for a more beautiful, perfect, mission accomplished, but we long for him each and every hour of every day.

One of my Facebook posts was this:

Every event that occurs in life counts, it may seem like "luck" or coincidence but there is no such thing as either. It only looks that way because we can't see the "big picture"...take each "event" good and challenging regardless of how large or small, as an integral part of your journey through life...to ensure that "big picture" ends up just as it was intended.

Chapter 8

"We hardly knew ye" "Number 76"!

"Jonathan, we hardly knew ye/ young as you seemed/but we'll know you in the eternity that will take eternity to comprehend" (Michael H. Brown, Jonathan's uncle who wrote and delivered his eulogy)

You, my friend, have taught me to live by faith, one day at a time.
Jonathan H. Miller
11-15-09
"I am thankful that in God's design, he made it so your path crossed mine." ♥ CP

I remember the saying "you know your child at home, teachers know them in school and the real them is somewhere in between". We always knew J to be a strong-willed, sociable child who embraced every new thing and every activity in a special way. We knew he was happy, we knew he loved his friends but until his death, we never knew the significant gifts that he had and how well he used each and every one of them. His mission in life was clear.

Boy, did we learn that through hearing the stories of J from his friends, teachers, employers and acquaintances. Did you ever stop and think about the fact that we seem to learn most about someone, only when serious illness or tragedy strikes? It is a shame we can't enjoy the total greatness about that person while they are with us.

A consistent theme will be that our J was always social and loved his friends. Being that he was always happy, we knew that his life was good. What we didn't know was that we had a son that was a significant blessing to everyone he met. He is described by strangers to us as his parents as a "special boy" and in such a way that the sincerity and depth of that person's expression is strongly felt.

Growing up, our children always knew we had a significant emphasis on the importance of loving people, respecting others, accept everyone for who they are and valuing relationships. Since J's death, we have learned that he "aced" this beyond what we could have expected. We often used to worry that J wasn't going to be rewarded for the strengths that he had, since they weren't athletic or academic. I am not sure if he would have ever, had he not died tragically where the students, teachers and administrators came together to reflect on his life to come to one conclusion. Such things expressed were that he was loved by all, one of the kindest people they knew, he had friends who crossed "all lines", and his death "devastated not only a student body but a community. We learned that J touched strangers in "mysterious" ways; as such stories were told when his death was announced.

J had the ability to make everyone feel as if they were his best friend, and so many kids came to us to say just that "I loved J Mill, he was my best friend". They all felt that way because that was the kind of genuine love J had for everyone. He had a heart of gold. All the good that he did was quiet and powerful. Isn't that how it should be?

J was the person that was always there to lend a helping hand. Whether it be his mother, father, sisters, grandparents, aunts, uncles, cousins, employers or friends. Everyone was important to him. Their needs always were more important than his, and he was the epitome of selfless, loyal, loving kid who understood "kindness" and "charity" better than anyone I have ever known.

Throughout the first week of learning of his death, the students sent us personal letters highlighting what J meant to them. As previously mentioned, in school, he was "J-Mill." We learned that he was the spirit of the class, the light in any room, the funny one, the one who always made someone feel better, the person always there to give a hug, the teammate who helped pick up the pieces after many disappointing losses, the one who cheered on the stronger athletes proud of their every move, even though he hardly had playing time. As his football coach said about J: "I would take a whole team of him" speaking of his spirit, character and hard work. As a matter of fact, his character was so valued, that his football number was retired, a number that will be displayed with initially only two others, one of which is a retired NFL player. J rarely played and rarely started if he did. It wasn't about athletics, but it was for a life well lived and important to all that he encountered. As his parents, we couldn't be happier at what number **"76"** stands for from this point on. After all, this is what we value and our dear son knew it and mastered it!

There are many that are devastated by this death for the many reasons that were expressed. J's life was the epitome of what we all need to understand is important in life.

Chapter 9

A life lived that "mastered kindness"

"*The standard for the love of God is giving all. It reaches into the very depths of the powers of your soul. When you are kind, you put others in the place of yourself. Self-love is naturally kind. Kindness is coming to the rescue of others when they need help. The very attempt to be like Jesus is already a source of sweetness within you, flowing with an easy grace over all who come within your reach.*" *(Hidden Power of Kindness; Lawrence G. Lovasik)*

"In the future I can't wait to see, if you'll open up the gates for me, till the day we meet again, in my heart is where I'll keep you friend"

R.I.P. J-Mill, you had the Heart of a Lion (Hoss)

When we speak of kindness many things come to mind. But if we seek to understand true kindness and what God expects of us, we learn that the term means so much more than most people think. In a book titled "The Hidden Power of Kindness" by Lawrence G. Lovasik, I have found that the way J lived his life included several examples of true "kindness." Many parts of this book describe J, specifically how he was able to love where love was needed, treated everyone as if they were his best friend and they felt that, respected everyone and their differences, sought to find peace in each and every day.

He served as an instrument of peace his entire life.

It wasn't until after J's death, that we began to understand the life that he led. Kindness, compassion and love for everyone that was mastered completely. This was especially evident through hundreds of letters written by his fellow classmates indicating, "J was my best friend," by so many. How can one person make so many feel they really are his "best friend"? God gave J a gift to show a community not what to do, but how to do it. How to master the basics of what God wants us all to be. Kind, loving one another, nonjudgmental, and that was J. Loyal, dedicated and always just a call or hug away from making a day better for someone.

"It only takes one smile to offer welcome, it only takes one moment to be helpful, it only takes one joy to lift a spirit, it only takes one life to make a difference, blessed be the person who will give it" ...A. Bradley

J had a way of knowing just what you needed

Excerpts from his friends to follow told us as much.

J would anticipate your needs and act accordingly. J would never turn away a request for help. Rather he would offer the help, often to help where it required hard labor or if it was out of his way. The desire to help others so willingly supports the part of his character that was charitable. Be it his friends calling him in the early morning hours to pick them up from a situation they wanted help in or his family member calling on him to stop by and help with something, there he was with that warm, big smile.

J was a gentle person and, as we have learned, attracted all people young and old. Stories from complete strangers of J's random acts of kindness were rampant. He just knew what was needed and took care of situations.

One woman mentioned that her child was crying and carrying on in a store and wanted something done. She indicated that J responded to the child very quietly, resulting in a calmness over the child. He grabbed what he went in the store for and quietly left. She never forgot that, and once J died, she told the storeowners about this encounter. They in turn told me.

J would never refuse hours that his employer needed him, despite the fact that at times he would work 12 hours, some of it requiring heavy lifting.

After a winter storm, J heard of our pastor's family's house being somewhat disrupted requiring clean up. That day, he spent hours with his dad cleaning up his parents' yard. The owners sent money, which he quickly turned around and gave to charity. His response was that he didn't do that for money. Every holiday, J looked forward to delivering food baskets for the St. Vincent de Paul society. He became an honorary member of the St. Vincent DePaul society after his death. He had been too young to be a member.

Love where love is needed

Every Christmas, as we would go see our "friend" in the nursing home, J would be sure he was there for the decorating of the tree and family holiday night. This "friend" is someone that has no one and we adopted years ago. She so looked forward to "her little buddy" coming and joining her for this party. As a matter of fact, our friend, whose name was Gerty, had J's picture as the only one on her bulletin board in the nursing home. After his death, she had the clipping of his obituary. On her deathbed, as I was called to be with her, being her only "family," it was only once a nun asked me to tell her to go see my son that she let go of this life. She lingered many days with no food or drink, just an occasional tear streaming down her face. The nun was right. J was there waiting for her, I believe, and off she went to her eternal life. Gerty's family left her side, but our gift was to add her to our family and how enriching it was for all of us.

**Pictured above, J, Gerty, and me.
Celebrating Christmas "family
night" at the nursing home.**

Many describe J as having a strong "conscience." I have learned that every kind action works to restore us, and help us balance right and wrong. J seemed to master this as a natural part of simply how he lived his life.

We have seen that kindness has a powerful influence on others. The dedications, the sadness, the outpouring of love to us and the endless stories about who J was to others, shows us that really, it was all about "kindness." So many were amazed by the person he was and how he touched so many lives in such a short time. The "gentle giant" as so many described him. A pastor friend of mine said to me "good begets good."

School aides and monitors often described J as someone "special." One school monitor approached me and wanted to let me know the type of person J was at school. She then opened a prayer book and a picture of J was inside it, and she said, "He and I pray together every day." She also mentioned that she talks to other kids about following his example.

NEVER UNDERESTIMATE THE ACT OF KINDNESS

So many people were so blown away by the tributes to my son. Those who experienced a record- breaking attendance (as expressed by the elder owner of the popular local funeral home) at his wake as well as his funeral mass. Such attendance provided many the ability to see firsthand what was behind the J they knew and loved, and that being his religion and love of God. Many have mentioned to me through emails, cards and in person to say, they really are considering going back to church again as J's funeral was powerful and inspiring. Some have mentioned that they weren't in a formal religion but now see that maybe they should be. Many others simply mentioned how all of the love for J and our family made them feel and recognized that really, it is about kindness. Many have said that J's life changed them forever, those I am referring now are the random adults, and many, many of his peers have said the same. They just see now how you need to live to really make a difference.

One of J's friend's moms took me to lunch to just mention how her son has been forever changed. She mentioned that her son was struggling and trying to come to grips with J's death. He couldn't understand why being so good, he had to die so soon. She stated that as he worked through this, the pain of losing J was manageable by recognizing that God only takes those that are truly good and by their death, it shows others the example they have set and how you need to live. Basically, it was the "only the good die young" idea. For a young person, that was a very profound expression and when we "believe," we know, God takes us when our mission is over.

So through J's life and through J's death, he is encouraging others to be kind, always. Kindness always warms our hearts. We know this through the kindness so many have shown to us as a grieving family. "It sweetens sorrow and lessons pain." We have realized the beauty in people. So many people.

Many do not realize the value of kindness. The life of J has made this front and center. It showed people that acting kindly truly does have value. So many experienced this through knowing how J lived and now through his death, have seen how important kindness was to so many.

According to L. Lovasik, "Kindness is the grand cause of God in the world. Where it is natural, it must be supernaturally planted. Your mission in life should be to re-conquer for God's glory His unhappy world and give it back to Him. Devote yourself to the beautiful apostolate of kindness, so that you and others may enjoy the bliss of the Divine Life". Become a member of the "Fraternity of Kindness". All it takes is an attitude that makes living in this manner the priority in your life."

Getting along with so many different types of people was such a dominant trait of Jonathan's that everyone noticed, and it became extremely obvious through the support and showing of everyone as they paid their respects. I believe J was successful with this for many reasons. We emphasized in our household that you need to love everyone – you can if you try. Differences in people are to be valued and learned from, not insulted. No one is better or lesser of a person than you. J would give in to others in order to keep balance and peace as long as it didn't cross the line with his own beliefs and better judgment, as many of his friends would share that about him. I recall one of the mothers of an acquaintance of J's said that her son called her sobbing and asking "why would God take such a great kid"? As life would play out, this same young boy died in a car accident a few years after J.

Jonathan Radiated Cheerfulness

"The best accessory we can "wear" is a smile."

Another common description of Jonathan was that he was always happy. He would always make others happy. So many people, young adults and old would say that on their darkest days, they would seek J out. Often all they needed was his warm smile or that big hug that he was always willing to share.

One day, a high school monitor approached me with tears in her eyes.

"One day," she said. "I was sad and couldn't smile, Jonathan came by and asked why I wasn't smiling and I said I just didn't feel like it, and J said with his warm, convincing smile: 'smile, it will be okay.'"

Then, he left. For whatever reason, the confidence and delivery of his positive responses always worked for those in need. Maybe it was divine guidance to help that person, most of us believe that was J's primary purpose. It was simply the way he lived, and he was always there for everyone. Being cheerful, he regularly lifted the spirits of so many, and people were drawn to this contagious joyful and peaceful person.

Sincerity was also obvious to those who knew him. Although the death of Jonathan can easily put us in despair, we keep our eye on the target. Someday we want to be with him again, and in order to do that, we have to live the way God wants us to, and that is to be cheerful with hope. Although our lives on earth bring us many challenges and sufferings, keeping our eye on the target, Heaven, and trusting God, provides us with the strength to carry on each day. Smiling through our pain. Seeking joy once again.

Chapter 10

FACING CHALLENGES AND TURNING THEM INTO SUCCESSES

Talk about turning lemons into lemonade...

J faced the sorrows and struggles he had with courage, confidence, and patience. He had many struggles and rather than letting them get him down, he found a way to make a joke about his shortcomings or just doing the best he could and enjoying the camaraderie with those who he loved, his peers. J never took life too seriously, especially himself. Failures were in the past, and he just knew how to move forward despite them. Taking problems in stride and moving on just came naturally.

Using this courage is how we are moving forward with our struggle of losing Jonathan. We needed to rebound like he would have, and we needed to show courage as he did. We have to spread this strength and courage to others who know what we are dealing with, handling the ultimately pain and sorrow, with as much grace as God gives us to do so.

I have learned that action helps me move forward when hit with struggles. Action encourages me to keep going. It helps me come to grips with my reality: the problems and pain do not disappear but rather it helps solve them and provide some hope for other joy and contentment to balance a shattered heart.

At a sermon during Lent one year, a priest said "you cannot get the crown unless you first carry the cross." Knowing that our struggles and sacrifices are for the sake of God and that He will provide us with peace and strength to get through this, it makes it become more worthwhile rather than focused on the loss and the sadness felt every day. Accepting God's will, although the challenge of a lifetime losing my son, freed me of some of the weight of the "cross" that I now have to carry. Cheerfulness and peace come with knowing that I am carrying on the way God wants me to do so. I have had to learn to rise above self and accept sacrifice and disappointments as crosses I am asked to carry. I know that I can't follow my own wills but make good of the wills of God. I pray always for the grace to carry the crosses despite my sadness or aversion to them. I find happiness in what I can bring to others so they are happy.

Here are some fundamental concepts that help us live better lives:

- Avoid passing judgment on others

- Resist greed in all its forms

- Control anger

- Learned to bear others offenses with kindness

- Recognize the consequences of unkind thoughts (J would avoid saying things or doing things that would offend or hurt another person. He was sensitive and became easily upset, to the point of tears, if he felt he did so.)

- Through death we see the transforming powers of J's kindness

- Use kindness when "correcting" others

- Cultivate a love that overflows in kind deeds

- Perform many works of mercy

As a son he was a joy: fun, loving, caring and always there for me. We were pals; we were grocery shopping buddies, coffee buddies, chats in the hot tub, having our nightly chats in my bedroom. J never went through the "terrible teen years" as his respect for us as parents was always there. NEVER missing a curfew, always regretting mistakes he made and showing his respect and love for us always. His easy-going spirit, his beautiful smile, and his love for his family are so sorely missed. "Why did he have to leave us so soon?" is the question that constantly comes up in our weakest moments.

Our hearts have holes so large it is beyond description. Our every minute has thoughts of the loss of this beautiful soul. Somehow we are challenged with honoring his legacy and spirit, showing a smile amidst extreme pain and sorrow, picking up those who are saddened around us by their burdens. We do so by showing strength, that "somehow" is coming to each of us. Improving our character in order to be sure we emulate the beauty that has become so well known about our dear son and brother.

Coping with a loss of this nature is indescribable, but one thing we know is the beauty, kindness, love and support shown to us is sustaining us. We live one moment at a time, and a day seems too long at times.

The fact that we are still moving forward, working hard, smiling when we can and keeping sincere to our faith shows the power of the Almighty. The love for a child is so deep that the loss would not be possible to endure without divine intervention. We thank God every minute for providing us the strength to carry on with grace and dignity.

Chapter 11

TRAGEDY MAKES OTHERS FEEL VULNERABLE

A death of this magnitude, with so much attention and as far reaching as it was, permeated this community for years. When a child dies suddenly, it is impossible to comprehend, especially a sudden, unexplainable death. Let's face it: one minute we are eating with them and talking about their plans for the day, and in our case his future, and hours later, he is gone forever. Gone without any ability to say goodbye, to remind him of our love, to hold him once again. No more laughter, goofing around, sweaty socks all over the house, clothes all over his room. The house immediately filled with deafening silence and empty despite those of us left here. At times it feels as though this is a bad dream that we just haven't awoke from yet. Please let us awake from this nightmare!

It is the everyday things about J that are so sorely missed. J lived his life with a lot of activity. He was often referred to as the "bull in the china shop," so miss that around the house. Sudden loss provides no preparation, resulting in the same feeling of a parent losing any child, but what I have learned is that the grieving for a sick child occurs upon diagnosis and the death, less a shock, however the separation very similar and just as painful.

The sudden nature of J's death has left so many feeling vulnerable. So many other parents so uncomfortable, not knowing what to say, almost fearing the same could happen to them. Is it catchy? Sometimes you feel others feel that way, odd as it may seem.

People can be awkward and say things that are offensive without meaning to do so. Everyone who knew him, knew him to be responsible and there was no "reason" for this untimely death, nothing for any of us to grab on to, making the acceptance that much more difficult. Did God turn his back for a moment and allow a very wrong thing to happen to our child? That was my mother's take on it. Feeling that God made a mistake despite knowing God makes NO mistakes.

God's role, although unclear of course, seems to be one that simply provides some young people to the "reward" of death earlier than many others. They are chosen because their mission has been so well accomplished at such a young age. Keeping such "chosen" children on earth would bring them struggles that they will be forever spared of, now in Heaven. My dad found consolation with J's death saying that he will never suffer - what a perfect life. The wisdom of my dad; this is true in so many ways.

We have found that many of our friends and acquaintances are visibly pained by our loss. I am sure they feel for us, but beyond that, they feel that if it could happen to us it could happen to them. That strips us as humans of our security and comfort level with life. Here is a good boy, who many knew personally to be that, and look what happened. Bad things really do happen to good people OR is it that we consider death "bad" because it hurts us on earth, but really "only the good die young"? I am beginning to believe the latter.

I know the pain as his mother and the negativity that results from missing him, but then I think about how he lived his life and the lives he changed and somehow it makes some sense. Our loss of a long life with our son was at the expense of meeting his mission early, positively impacting others and changing lives. Is that negative? I dare say not and I wouldn't want it any other way. God blessed us with the privilege of having J, even if only for seventeen years. Most people don't have the blessing of a child of this nature ever. We are amply blessed!

A family that loves beyond the word.

Not only do we have the support of a community, but most significantly is the love and support we have from our family. J's aunts, uncles and cousins are very close. Their sense of loss is deep, their support and love for us is so comforting. The sad part of this is that due to the love for J, there are far too many people hurting. It is one thing to deal with your own pain, but it is hard to watch others suffer as well.

A particularly sad scenario is watching his grandparents suffer. They have had two tragedies, watching their child suffer and having lost a grandchild. We all know that life isn't supposed to work out this way, but old people die, not healthy, loving and good children! This type of death makes others feel vulnerable. Especially when the person is one with a "stellar reputation." It makes many doubt God's plan, doubt their faith and angry about the great loss they feel. Until my mom's last day, she never truly reconciled God's plan. She was the epitome of one of God's faithful servants as I saw her, but this challenge was beyond her acceptance. She would say that although God typically doesn't make mistakes, He did by taking J so young. I know now that she is in Heaven with him, she fully understands. I used to remind her of what she always taught me and that is to trust in God's plan regardless.

Chapter 12

HOW DO WE RECONCILE WITH GOD'S PLAN?

Sometimes our sole purpose is to take the "bullets" with grace. It's tough, but "what doesn't kill you will make you stronger." We know this all too well!

I can't begin to express the number of people, who to this day, look at me with those "puppy dog" eyes (which I might add, I am not fond of) and ask, "how do you do this?". How quickly they hear about God's work in our lives! I just have no other way to describe my life.

So first we have to remind ourselves of God's role in our lives. It is not to control our behaviors and actions but to support us and strengthen us when we need it most. Free will has made life on earth very challenging and a struggle. Everyone has and will struggle in this life. It is all about the faith that we have in God to get us through that will make the difference in how we move through it. It isn't easy to trust God immediately because of the anger related to the loss of a child. But when we reflect again, we have to remember that God didn't cause the death, but honored it because J had fulfilled his mission. Had he not, he would not have died. We all have a mission and purpose, when we are through, God will call us home.

God is all-knowing. Our suffering is God's suffering. God wants us all to live as he guides us in order for the best results. None of us live in a manner consistent with this direction completely. That reflects our flaws as people. At times, this poor direction has significant negative consequences. The problem with this thought is this does not support the reason for J's death. He did NOTHING wrong. It was a medical condition that never showed up and would not have in time to save his life as a doctor once told me. It was just his time.

We know that God can stop a tragedy and so one would say: why didn't he stop this one? The answer keeps going to the fact that J had completed his mission. He earned his "ticket" to Heaven, although at a young age, it is a "congratulations" to him! We somehow need to see that and be happy for this accomplishment at such a young age.

Finding the blessings in tragedy is a challenge. A life of this nature in particular, since all anyone can see early on is the great loss we all have for the person in our lives that always made it better. Why would God take this type of person away from so many of us?

Every tragedy has in it a lesson to be learned. A life lived as beautifully as J's leaves a powerful legacy so he lives on in all of those who he touched. Sometimes it is only until someone is gone that we reflect on their life and their attributes. God has left us with a great deal to learn about the life of such a great kid!

THE SMILE OF AN "ANGEL"

At times it seems this is a figure of speech. As time passes, the description of J continues in many ways. The countless pictures he is in with his friends focuses on that ever--present, warm, loving, smile that he was well known for. He is being referred to as the "Angel of Lewiston Porter" as well as referred to at the Niagara University (NU) invocation for the beginning of school the year he was supposed to begin, "remember Jonathan Miller, the guiding angel of the class of 2014." Without fail, everyone that I encountered who knew him or of him mentions the common theme, he was "special," he was kind, and he had a beautiful warm smile. So many mentioned how having a bad day would turn, just when they would see J, be it in the hallway or passing him in the coffee shop he visited daily.

God intended J to be an angel on earth. Weird as that may sound to many, I have had to learn to accept that this is the reality of his journey. God provided J with the uncanny ability to be not only "liked" but loved and fondly remembered, even if he was a mere acquaintance to others. People admired his ability to look at life as happy, peace-filled and sure worth living, which makes his death even more difficult. How could God believe that it was time to take a person who had this much impact, to so many people away so young? That is the million-dollar question and one that we may never have an answer to. Ever.

The tributes continue for J at school. Windows show "In loving memory of J-Mill," wristbands, and a specific site on Facebook, so anyone who desires can write a message. The mural painted in his honor in the entrance lobby area of his high school is fantastic. J had a joke going that the school store was "his" store, so the store is now painted with the sign "J-Mill's" store and then inside has his forever football jersey number "76" which was, as mentioned, retired in Fall 2010. The Senior Lounge was named after J, as he was instrumental in getting that room remodeled as such.

While I gave away a lot of J's clothing quite early after his death, we did save some special T-shirts. They were turned into a huge, beautiful quilt coordinated by J's sisters and given to Kevin and me. What a treasure. We keep this quilt in our family room, and it brings us smiles of better days!

Much power comes from those in Heaven with Jesus, who guides them to do their work as He desires, now more powerfully, now from Heaven.

J's cousins Rob and Joe were like big brothers to J and loved him so much that they even used his name as the middle name for their first-born sons, Ryan Jonathan Cacace and Robert Jonathan Jenkins, who forever carry the love and peace of J's spirit through his name and will carry with them throughout their lives. J loved kids and I know he would adore all of his baby cousins. This is Ryan Jonathan with J's guitar. I figured J would love his first cousin to have his namesake to have his favorite guitar.

Pictured above is Ryan Jonathan
with his sweet sister Vanessa.

I speak of all the learning through this process. Some of what we were experiencing we didn't recognize as anything other than moving forward. Others see it quite differently.

Resilience is a gift from God.

As a student at Columbia University, J's cousin Chrissy saw that Scientific Magazine was seeking someone who showed resilience with the loss of a child. Chrissy contacted me to see if I would do the story. Knowing this is an important message for others in the healing process, I agreed to do so. We have had the benefit of this gift of resilience. The story covered aspects that would allow others to fully understand how I was getting through this while seeking to become "whole" again.

My response, as you have to know by now is that it's all about God, It's all about J's life, and it's all about the people who surround us with love and compassion. That's about it!!

A photographer from this magazine came to take a picture at the tree where his SUV stopped that evening he journeyed to Heaven and then pictures in J's bedroom, which is still intact for the most part.

Again, his legacy gets larger and lives on and on. That's how it should be. God insists on it. We love it!

Chapter 13

THE LIVES HE CHANGED WITH ONLY SEVENTEEN YEARS

"It is because the human spirit knows, deep down, that all lives intersect. That death doesn't just take someone, it misses someone else, and in the small distance between being taken and being missed, lives are changed" (The Blue Man).

This was in a yearbook next to a picture of one of J's childhood friends as her quote "in loving memory of Jonathan H. Miller" RD

Hundreds of letters that we received stated over and over how much the way he loved and lived, have influenced the way they will try to live their lives. It is often only once someone dies that people "feel" the loss and see the impact that one beautiful life had.

Message to me on Facebook…"Joyce Meyer Ministries- One person can make an unbelievable difference —Joyce - This is your Jonathan" (KV)

"So in summation I don't even know who you racin'
I'm already at the finish line with the
flag wavin' (lifelong friend DB)"

"The world will little note nor long remember what
we say here, but it can never forget what they did
here"
"It's not what you take when you leave this world
behind you, it's what you leave behind you when
you're gone." BY

"Prayin' waiting on you, To run back through that
door, To the way it was before you left. It wasn't
long enough together, but it was long enough to last
forever."
"LIVE LIKE YOU WERE DYING" J-MILL LOVE
AND MISS YOU MC

"Jeannine when my son told me Jonathan always
would say "Live by faith one day at a time" it reminded
me of my childhood when I would tell family and
friends to have faith and take life day by day. I
continue to try to instill that into my children and
those I associate with. Awesome words of wisdom,
from a wonderful young man." DV

Jll: "I was personally going to speak of Jonathan in my
words to the freshmen at the Freshmen Convocation.
The Invocation at the Convocation included a
beautiful remembrance of Jonathan expressing he
was to attend N.U. in the Fall and died unexpectedly.
All attending were asked to pray for the family of
Jonathan. Class of 2014's Special Angel. I continue

to keep Jonathan's memorial card on my conference table. As I sit there each day with others, I always ask Jonathan to help and guide N.U. and myself. "

THE SPIRIT OF 76 SCHOLARSHIP

It isn't how much money you make or how well you do in school academics, but what matters is how you made others feel that will last a lifetime.

Kevin and I created the "Spirit of 76 Memorial Scholarship" to ensure J's memory was solidly embedded in the fabric of the school he loved so dearly. This scholarship was to be provided to a deserving senior student who lived in a manner consistent with how others knew J lived. They had to be nominated by anyone who recognized such qualities in them, then they write a response as to why they should be considered. The focus is on being kind, compassionate and helping others.

J simply changed lives in many ways. One particular .student that was nominated for the Spirit of 76 Scholarship for the first year of the award stated some profound facts about his relationships with J, how J changed his life and how he impacted his life forever.

A student wrote this, in response to his nomination for the scholarship: "When I was young, I was a "loser". When J came to our school, I felt that maybe I would have a chance impressing the new kid and he wouldn't see me as a loser. As it turned out, J didn't need convincing, and he liked me for who I was. I couldn't believe when he invited me to his birthday party. I finally felt worthy and not so much of a loser. J gave me confidence in myself as time went on. We played sports together, and even though neither of us were very strong athletes I stayed because of his perseverance. I am not sure I would have continued with sports had it not been for the inspiration and example J set by keeping at it despite the role on the team."

This same person stated that he felt that the characteristics J had were those that he admired and chose to follow. He will continue to live the life as J did focusing on kindness, selflessness and perseverance. By J's example, it became clear that this is the way to live and it matters, a whole lot!"

This scholarship alone resulted in over $10,000 given to deserving students.

Chapter 14

MESSAGES FROM HEAVEN ....Are you "listening"?

Life takes us unexpected places. Such places are meant to teach us something but it is up to us to "listen" to the message. When you become sensitive to the importance of living in the "now," living in the moment, this begins to make more sense. Life experiences become more and more important in taking in our environment when we truly believe that each and every encounter is meant to teach us something.

As I have been on this journey, I spend a lot of quiet time. I am very reflective, as you can imagine, given the content of this journey written throughout this book. I do indeed live in the moment.

I have learned all too well that life is not to be taken for granted. This has made me highly aware of each and every moment. Actually living in the moment is something that has allowed me to cope as well as I have been able to. I deal with the here and now and don't allow my feelings or sadness preoccupy my every second. I have learned to value the small and large moments of life.

In the course of this change, becoming more aware leads to incredible experiences. One such experience is how the spiritual world plays such an important role in our lives. I have become very sensitive to our spiritual world.

I want to share with you some of these profound experiences not only because they have helped me personally but also because sharing such experiences has helped so many others. Such experiences show us that love lives forever and that our loved ones never leave us. What am I saying here? I am suggesting that their spirit presents in other ways to provide what we need at any given time.

Earlier I talked about visionary dreams. Such dreams provided those who had them with the feeling of J's presence and resulted in peace in their mind and hearts. God knew what they needed!

I also previously talked about how "Heaven" provides us with thoughts and even clues that we need to consider. Remember J's sister's premonition? This was the evening of J's passing, right after he left the house, his older sister thought she heard that very loud, frightening crash.

Here are more powerful experiences. Coincidence? No way, there is no such thing!

I think most of us have heard the phrase "pennies from heaven," or unexplainable appearances of pennies. Well, the first several months, this was one of the experiences we all had. One night while going to sit out on the deck where we spent so much time with J, we found, on the coffee table, an old penny. When in Queensbury visiting relatives, as we were walking up to their door, there was a penny sitting on the cement near the door.

In the driveway of our home. On the floor of Lauren's room after cleaning it. Where do they come from?

This next experience was very overwhelming. After a day of deep sadness, and actually most of the day just cleaning and crying to get through it, I decided to go for a ride. I left a spotless home, and Kevin and I were the only ones living at home at this time. When I returned home, I still felt extremely sad. I looked at the countertop and on it was a half-eaten potato chip. Now, if you know me you would know, since J's passing, no snacks of this nature exist in our house. I shouted out to Kevin, who was working outside, asking if he had potato chips. He just laughed and said "no." So I sat to wonder, where did this come from? My meticulously clean house has a half-eaten potato chip. Then my heart skipped a beat. I had to realize that given the deeply sad state I was in, I was getting a message. Who ate chips? J of course. J was the one who had crumbs all over the house, socks everywhere, clothes randomly placed around the house at times. So the message was clear – well sort of. The result? An overwhelmingly peaceful feeling and heaviness lifted from my oppressively heavy heart.

How I miss his presence all around the house. I guess God knew that I would realize this was J, given the nature of this divine message. Whatever it was intended for, it gave me the peace for that day that I needed. My J was there.

One evening, a neighbor who also lost a son was visiting. Needless to say, we were struggling with our sadness as we relate to such agony. We were quietly having coffee and all of a sudden a loud noise in the corner of the room behind my neighbor sounded. We all stopped to find out what "fell" or what happened, even going in the garage to see if anything fell. There was nothing, so we just looked at each other and moved on, peaceful despite the "encounter." We knew it was intended to remind us of the presence of those who pass.

There are so many things that happen to remind us of eternal life and spirits among us. Specifically experiencing unusual spots of warmth or coolness and air passing over me from time to time. No open windows, no changes in room temps. Then the "scent" that was clearly one J possessed. We all have one that reminds others of us. This happened regularly for the first year.

What about electrical appliances going on, doorbells ringing at all hours of the night? Logic makes you feel that it is something wrong that requires more research. When we sought an electrician to see what was going on, he stated that nothing was wrong and he couldn't explain what was happening.

Well, of course not!

One night, the night before Alyssa was going to take the most crucial exam of her college career, the horn of her car went off. Kev went out to stop it, but the only way to stop it was to unplug the wires. I am guessing J was sending his "good luck" wishes! That never happened again, so we cancelled the appointment to check her car out. It seems it was an "isolated" incident.

One day my mother mentioned that she keeps seeing shadows of J's stature walking by her. In no way was he going to leave his Grandma Rose's side. They had a profoundly close bond.

One of my cousins came in from out of town, wanting to learn more about J and the unbelievable impact he had on his classmates. She actually went to the school to interview teachers, students and administrators to learn more. We chose J's room for her to stay in. What she encountered was incredible.

She woke up to tell us that she was fretting the day and wondering how she would be received. That night, she woke up about 4 a.m. to go to the bathroom, and then got back into bed still a bit nervous. All of a sudden, she felt this weight and arms wrapped around her. There were no words; she just finally got the peace she needed to know that all would be go well the next day. She said to us she knew it was our J. Everyone knew his big bear hugs!

Then J's aunt and cousin whom we gave J's wallet to found J's permit license inside it. When we gave it to him, I was sure it was empty as J left very little behind so I wanted to hold onto whatever I could. His cousin said to his mom "see J is always with me." This younger cousin was like the little brother he always wanted and didn't have. God knew he needed that.

One day I was up and down from the basement several times doing laundry, seeing the workout mat out and ensuring it was clean down there particularly due to guests coming to town. One visit down and I noticed the dogs were on the mat licking like crazy. I went over to it and saw it was pixie stick powder. Where did it come from? Oh well, I knew quickly, smiled, emptied it in the sink and moved on. J ate many of those in his day. My buddy always had food left downstairs! He hung out there often especially while I was working out. He was often by my side. Even if it was at night before going to bed and plopping his upper body over mine to just "be" together. Oh I would do anything for those moments again!

One night in mass, Kev and I were particularly struggling. The homily had one line in it that said something like "and your son appeared in the form of a dove," we both happened to look outside and sure enough, a dove was fluttering there most of that mass. We have not seen this again.

If it weren't for my own experiences, I am not sure I would necessarily grasp or appreciate these happenings. There are so many: there are messages God wants us to have, and there are ways God knows what your heart needs and amply provides. Believe the unexplainable. That is called FAITH.

Too often, when you feel you want to share such occurrences, you are cautious because you believe people will think you went a little crazy, or are hoping too much or whatever. Well that is simply not the case. There is no way I am looking for signs of anything, *My heart is speaking and God responds.*

Chapter 15

THEN THE FEATHERS!

Did you ever hear of white feathers coming from "nowhere"? Did you ever wonder what they meant? Now that I bring your attention to them, I bet you will also find them in the future. So many others have since they have followed my posts regarding such "miracles".

This was all new to me. I was so often perplexed but no doubt paused intently to determine how to make sense of coming across so many in such unusual places and unexpected times.

*"**Angel Feathers** are symbolic of angels considered to be the most divine and purest entity created by God. Angels symbolize the spreading love and sharing their purity in this hardcore world. The fact that they are not flesh and bones like normal living creatures of this world, in fact, they are made of pure light, their existence cannot be physically seen or felt like the normal beings. While they carry out their duty of spreading peace and love in this chaotic world, they leave behind traces of themselves for us to follow and believe in. " Padre from the Blog of Angels*

Feathers come in many colors. The color of feathers we find are white. I have learned that white feathers are to provide us with divine help without ever asking for it! But God knows our heart, our struggles, our sadness, and He provides us what we need for any given day. They are to grace us with peace and positivity, and such experiences in finding these have done just that. They also represent the successful journey of a departed soul from this world to Heaven. While I have read about feathers in many places, I would say that this is exactly what finding white feathers has meant to us, therefore, I related completely to such descriptions. The variety of colors each come with their unique "message." I would suggest that when and if you do encounter such "messages" you do so keeping in mind the feeling you get when such feathers appear. I believe whatever that feeling is, is exactly what you needed at that time. That's divine intervention!

The feathers have become the consistent "message" from J to us. Why white feathers? I would often ask myself this question. To me it is this. I came to the conclusion that I get such feathers so that it ties into J because the white dove is my image of J. Because of his peaceful spirit I see him more in the form of a carefree dove. The Holy Spirit Dove in particular, carefree and an instrument of peace and guidance. That's why I feel God sends feathers to symbolize that the message is from J, and such messages do provide us peace and guidance. I believe that it is God's way of drawing our attention to where the message is coming from.

So what about these feathers?

There are far too many instances to describe related to such "miracles," but let me try to provide a few. The same day I saw the half-eaten potato chip, I then walked upstairs and outside of J's bedroom was the first white feather I got. I was so confused. I had just cleaned, and there were no feathers in the house because J was allergic to them. Where did this come from? I almost threw it out, but "something" told me to pause, keep it and just be. The peace that came to me from this overwhelmingly sad day was certainly miraculous.

Then one evening, we were sitting watching TV in the family room and I happened to look at our black Yorki-poo dog and saw something white sticking out of his short curly fur. Yes, you guessed it, I pulled a sizable feather out of his fur. *What?*

Then there are countless times when a white feather appears, whether it be on my car seat, on our countertops, on my bed, on my desk or floating in front of me during a stressful time. I keep each and every one, but I could truly write a book just on this aspect of our journey.

I happened to tell my dad, who was a rather quiet, private type of guy, about these experiences. I was almost "afraid" to share them, wondering how people would view my description of events leading to find white feathers. My father quickly and firmly said, "God is sending you miracles. You must share them to show others how He interacts in our lives."

I started to do that and I can't begin to describe how much this has affected those on my social media channels. So many have said that they now get messages from their loved ones. Many who get white feathers actually credit J as coming their way in their time of need. My dad was right; to share such miracles with others inspires them to notice their own. This has been the case, and usually someone will write to me to share their "story."

Every November since his passing, we put up a gold tree covered with doves and white feathers, and we began this on the first anniversary of his passing. This celebration has become a positive experience for those who know about it. So much so that many people buy doves for the tree every year, and the ornaments have come in over the years by many of our friends and relatives to add to his tree. We often have celebrations on the anniversary of his death and this includes inviting others to come and place a dove on his memorial tree. This tree remains up through Christmas and removed until the following year. It's a peace-filled, beautiful memorial to J and serves as a reminder of all who love and support us through this journey.

Robert Jonathan bought J this ornament. This is Robby and I placing his ornament on the tree.

Chapter 16

NUMBER 76

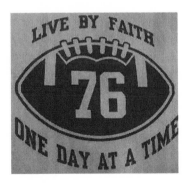

Throughout this book, I've talked about the number **76**, which is a number becoming so much a part of J's legacy, hence the title. This of course was his football jersey number. This number was retired, like mentioned, shortly after his passing. Being a significant number tying to J, we know that beyond feathers, divine messages come through to us using the number **76!**

So, what about it? Well, I want to say that so often this number "pops up" and of course makes us pause, and yes, we feel J's presence in whatever the situation might be. Coincidence? No absolutely not; there's no such thing.

So often we look at the temperature in the car, in the house, in the garage and just at that time, it happens to be **76** degrees. Naturally we always take note, and that's a "hello" from Heaven!

Then we embarked on planning Alyssa's wedding just this past year, 2019. I can't even tell you all of the connections that had this number in it. Whether it be deposits required, costs of various vendors or items; actually for her wedding when we inquired about having a sit-down dinner, they informed us that we could only have **76** if we choose to have the sit-down meal. Why not 75, 100, but **76**? We smile at such a "wink" from the Heavens. Further, the wedding was in Canada and the money exchange rate is, you guessed it, **76** every time we go to pay on something.

Actually, the draft of my journal had **76** pages! I noticed this as I worked on writing this book.

The first memorial golf outing had over 100 golfers signed up, but naturally a few fall off closer to the event, and on the day, there were **76!**

We could go on and on, but you get the idea. Watch for such signs from loved ones lost!

A community full of compassion and kindness

The tree planting dedication was another one of those heart-warming events that put a few more pieces of shattered hearts together.

On the day of this celebration, I wrote the following speech read by Alyssa:

"Once again, our Lew Port family gathered to show us support and kindness. The cross we have been given to bear has been made lighter by having them all here to help us carry this and join us on this journey.

We come together as a community, many of are unsure how to deal with the loss of Jonathan, but here together knowing, we have each other. We can remember that warm smile of Jonathan's, we can share memories and we can remember the lighthearted nature of J…hopefully bringing a smile and sense of peace to us all.

The planting of a tree is special. As Rabindranath Tagor put it: "Trees are the earth's endless effort to speak to the listening heaven". Planting a tree is a healing experience. When we see this tree it will forever provide us good memories of a life well lived. The **Flowering Pear tree** that is here today is a symbol of what our Lew Port family is all about and… what Jonathan was all about… and that is **affection and love**.

The memorial stone placed here will remind us that this is a special tree and has special meaning. It will remind us of why we loved Jonathan and the good times we had with him, many of them right here at this location.

The power of affection and love are immeasurable. We feel your **love,** we feel your **affection** and we thank you from the bottom of our hearts for walking this path with us. And so, we all remember how Jonathan lived his life and we all can do the same "live by faith, one day at a time."

There is significant comfort knowing that Jonathan, who was so special to many of us, will never be forgotten.

So let's hold tight to memories for comfort, leaning on each other for strength and remembering the gift of Jonathan's life and what he did for each of us who knew him. Memories live forever, and Jonathan lives forever.

We want to thank you all for being here…

God bless you all for your kindness, for your endless prayers and support, for your countless expressions of affection and love. You are all a part of our daily prayers and will hold a special place in our hearts forever."

Alyssa and I at the tree planted where after each football game, the team circles it and has a moment of silence, then shouts "J-Mill." He continues to be a symbol for each and every one of the players and coaches.

There were so many tributes.

Nothing is more important to parents losing a child than for them to be remembered. How will anyone know they lived dying so young is our worry. I would be sure most, if not all of us, feel the same feeling. One way to make this better is a tribute. Reminding all of a life lived, rather than the passing, is key. Memories that last forever are the most important ones.

The Frontier Golf Club memorial brick, NU Golf Team – team golf team bag tags "in memory of

Jonathan Miller," retired number for football at Lewiston Porter High School; Jonathan Miller Spirit of 76 Memorial Scholarship; the green and white memorial wristbands and window clings; the memorial bricks that are located in various places. One right in the heart of our wonderful village, and one of them at a beautiful lighthouse, one we visit every year.

Some of his friends even got tattoos. Kev, Lauren and Alyssa also got one and finally I did as well. There is something about that permanent reminder of such an amazing person. I got my tattoo just recently but it isn't the "family tattoo" below. Mine is the infinity symbol with a feather embedded in it and 'Faith' with three doves, one flying signifying J's earned his wings and how he "flew" away. Every part of it just as the one below has a powerful message embedded within it. It was placed on my underarm, just below the wrist so I can look at it all the time. I love it. I never thought I would ever get a tattoo. Never say never!

The Family Tattoo

J's dad posed for this family tattoo. Only he, Lauren and Alyssa have it. The Tattoo Artist "retired" the design once it was complete on each of them. Others wanted it, but it was reserved for our family. Frank Rotella Jr., the tattoo artist nailed it. Each and every part of it is symbolic of J. The cross is the tattoo cross J wanted when he turned 18. The "Live by Faith,

One Day at a Time" is the saying J is well known for. The doves, his retired jersey number, his faith, all represented right here!

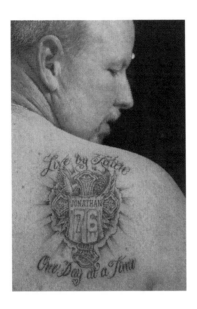

Then the school had his initials "JM" on ALL winter Varsity sports jerseys and senior sweatshirts/T-shirts.

We can't forget the Orange Cat Coffee shop logo created in his memory "Pour the Love" as well as the created coffee **"Blend 76".**

Mentions of him at important meetings held through the Niagara County legislature, town meetings, City hall meetings, St. Vincent DePaul Society as well as the Niagara Falls Board of Education. All having moments of silence and speaking to the loss for our communities of such a loved, great kid overall.

J's employer at the time, Brickyard BBQ Restaurant, originally started the golf outings. This memorial fund, over the years, resulted in creating a larger fund. To date over **$70,000** has been given in J's name to local charities and to a Lew Port Senior through the Spirit of 76 Scholarship.

The picture above includes J's
uncles and cousins.

*Whatever the gesture, it has been permanently
placed in our hearts. We are grateful.*

Chapter 17

THE HEART OF
THE SCHOOL – AN
INSTRUMENT OF
PEACE - NOW GONE

A month or so after J's death, I got a call from a school administrator saying kids at school were fighting, not getting along, feeling "alone," and experiencing major conflict among those who used to be friends-friends even split apart. After thinking through it, they believed that not having J there had caused the conflicts. I learned that J had a way of keeping all types of kids together getting along, despite their personality differences. J loved all and wanted everyone to be friends. J kept everyone together in his quiet way. Some of them were seeking guidance from school personnel.

How does one quiet life make such a HUGE difference? What is God telling us through J, what does He want us to learn from this pain and sorrow so many feel?

As his mother, I knew him as my son, and it is only through hearing such comments to follow that I fully understood just who he was.

J's friends have described him as "different than the rest of us" and one further went on to say, "it may sound weird but I feel that he was an angel on earth." This was compelling coming from young teenage boys.

One friend told his mother that after coming from the mausoleum and reflecting "with" J in spirit, he came to a conclusion and said "I think God takes only the good ones young. God does this to show the rest of us how we need to live. J did that, he changed so many of us."

J frequented a popular coffee shop in town. Being a regular, many people encountered him daily. The owners wanted to share some of their observations and sentiments about J and his interactions with all they witnessed him to encounter:

"J had charisma that was incredible; people who didn't even know his name were sobbing and continue to talk about him."

They further went on to say "the village and town was under a dark cloud the week of his death; the community continues to want to show their love to the family."

Inspired by J and the legacy he left ended up creating a coffee blend they call "Blend 76," which ties back to his retired football jersey number. Further, they created a logo that reflected his life and is called "Pour the Love." They strongly felt J was the epitome of sharing his love.

The tree that J's SUV hit, to us, is a reminder of his journey on to eternal life. Kev, his dad made a white cross for it. Kevin lovingly repaints it each season, touching, beautiful, so heartfelt; now nailed to "the tree." It remains a positive, peaceful reminder to all who pass the tree of J's life.

THE CEREMONIAL DOVES ON JUNE 25…J'S EIGHTEENTH BIRTHDAY!

To celebrate the one who has died is an important part of healing, and this particular celebration was so powerful.

One of J's beloved teachers had a Catholic mass to celebrate J's eighteenth birthday, and that was also graduation day. We decided to send off ceremonial doves afterward, as the dove is our reminder of the life he led, a symbol of hope, peace and love and may move us along the grieving process. Releasing J completely to God was the hard part, but maybe felt this was one step to healing.

What a beautiful way to start what could have been the hardest day since the day J went to eternal life! But instead, it was as sad as it was joyful. Once again, we had a full church to be there to wish our J a first birthday in heaven and to celebrate letting him go and be at peace in spirit; to guide us the rest of our lives on earth. We did this by letting go a ceremonial dove and three angel doves. The music played was beautiful and I am sure J's message to us: "If You Could See Me Now"(Bishop Paul Morton), this song focuses on the peace and happiness that one enjoys once they get to heaven. They want us to know that they don't want to return. They are "walking streets of gold and standing tall and strong"… "Borrowed Angels" (Kristin Chenoweth) was also played. This focused on the feelings of so many discussed throughout this book who felt J was an angel on earth and we know he is now.

His friends, teachers, parents of his friends, other adults in his life, felt he was different than any of us. He was full of grace, peace, kindness and love. He radiated that and it was just who he was. He touched lives in ways we never knew. "There must be borrowed angels here in this life."

J's sisters opened the doors to release the doves below.

Chapter 18

The Journey of Strengthening Faith

The "new" normal. The "new" happy. The "new" joyful life.

I am asked constantly: how are you doing this?

Many are amazed at how well I am doing, and "how can this be?" is what I used to think.

My heart is less heavy. I find peace, I laugh and I enjoy some things again.

The answer came very clear to me fairly early on. The answer to all of these questions are simply, first, my faith. I know God. Really, I do feel that close to God. This type of emotional turmoil forced me to find a source of strength and hope. I didn't need to look far. I am close to God and He is clearly with me always.

From a young age, we prayed as a family and learned that that is how you find your peace, comfort and guidance. What a gift from my parents – the gift of faith. There is absolutely nothing more powerful.

As a result, I became a strong prayer warrior – doing novenas, regularly saying the rosary and having a particularly strong dedication to the Blessed Mother. This belief that we are being protected and knowing that we can do whatever it is we are "asked" to do provides a strong foundation for coping with difficulties. I strongly believe that we only get what we can handle in life. Some people hate to hear this, but if you truly believe in God's role in our lives, it sparks a confidence that is needed to handle struggles. I have several life events that have made this very clear.

I also reflect on the positive life I had with my son. There are no regrets, and this is important to moving through this process. We had a strong, positive bond and had tremendous fun together. There were no "I wish we did" or "I shouldn't have done" etc. He knew daily, often several times a day, how much I loved him through words and actions. There is also, like I've mentioned, tremendous love and support from our family and the community. All of these things are the answers to "how I do it." The power of prayer, positive thoughts and kindness, living life with purpose and focus, loving those around you – these are all critical to the healing process.

I also know that God is expecting those of us suffering most to send a powerful message of His love in our lives. Through our actions, our smiles through our pain, our getting our lives back to our "new" normal amazes people. This witness to God's role in our life inevitably brings them closer to God. They can see His work through us. How else would we be doing it? You do not suffer a loss of this magnitude and move through in a healthy manner on your own. God is present, always.

I mentioned earlier that I have had some trials that have brought me closer and closer to God and to understand his role in my life. There have been some powerful "unexplainable" occurrences in my life that can be explained only one way, as **divine intervention**.

What brings us to know God more clearly?

Over thirty years ago, my husband and I moved back to my hometown. We were having our first baby, and we wanted the baby to be close to family. We left our jobs and started all over, and we moved in with my parents to get our feet on the ground.

One late morning our baby was napping. She didn't sleep well, so we were always told to let her cry to sleep. We often tried to do that, but this one morning I heard the cry on the intercom and *"something told me"* to go get her. So I did. I went up to get her out of her crib and came downstairs. Earlier a neighbor asked to see the baby. Now that Lauren was up, I decided I would walk her over to the neighbor's house. Within minutes fire trucks were at our home. A fire began right at the head of her crib, from the window air conditioner. My brother was home at the time and heard "crackling" on the baby monitor. When he went to check on her, the flames were pouring out of the room. My dear daughter would have perished in that fire had I not gotten her this one time when I was "nudged" to do so. God "telling" me? Yes, that is my feeling.

The house was destroyed. We were displaced. It had to be rebuilt. But it was a house, not a person, so becoming extremely grateful was first on my mind. Needless to say, I dropped to my knees thanking God for sparing me this child. My first conversion moving closer to God began then, 31 years ago. I began to go to daily mass. I felt I needed to show God that I am grateful and devoted to Him in any way I can.

Years passed, two more blessings later, two more children were born. We had a beautiful family life.

Touched by an angel

One evening, now seventeen years after the fire, this same daughter, our first-born had another near-death experience. This time it was a near fatal car accident. The dreaded phone call came to us to tell us our daughter had been in an accident and she was seriously hurt but would live. I was very perplexed that the caller knew so much and had such a calming way about her that it naturally made me calm down despite this news. I wanted to get her phone number in case I lost her as she was with my daughter at the scene. When I asked for the phone number of the person who called me she said "you won't be able to call me but if I lose you I will call you back." Further, I asked her if she was a nurse and she stated "no." How did she know Lauren would be okay? I then asked the person who called me where the accident occurred, and she stated "I am not sure. I am not from around here", sparking further mystery. As it turned out, I didn't lose contact with her and kept her on the phone until we were well on our way to the hospital.

We were sent to the local trauma hospital in Buffalo, New York. Kevin and I met the ambulance at the trauma center at the hospital. Our Lauren was "broken" head to toe and truly it was overwhelming to know she had survived once details of the accident came about. While waiting in the ER waiting room, the EMT came out to see us as we were not able to stay with Lauren given the magnitude of her injuries. While the EMT was just trying to tell us what happened, I quickly stopped him and asked, "who was the lady with my daughter?"

He looked perplexed at me and said "there was no lady."

I then insisted there was and told him she called me.

"I'm sorry Mrs. Miller," he said. "But there was no way a lady could have been with your daughter."

Confused and wondering but having more to think about at this critical time, I went on to thank him for staying with Lauren since we couldn't be with her given her injuries.

A day later, in the hospital out of a sound sleep, my Lauren wakes up sobbing. I jumped up to see what hurt her.

"Mom," she said. "Did a lady call you?"

"Yes," I replied.

"I don't think she was real," she said. "No one could have fit in the car with me and when I saw her all of my pain and fear was gone. She was with me until I got into the ambulance."

I actually tried to find the number on our caller ID to thank this woman. When I asked my son to look at the calls that night, all of them were there but this call. Perplexing. Pondering. Confusing. It seemed to be obvious this was another one of God's angels, although this one wasn't in full person, only Lauren and I experienced this woman. No other person saw her at the scene.

Lauren, as an artist, created an image of what this woman looked like. Lauren then described this woman as looking like a friend of mine who was a nun. My friend asked me about this encounter and I told her what Lauren had said.

With tears in her eyes, she said, "Jeannine, my mom is known to come to people in accidents, and she strongly resembles me."

Angels are sent to earth!

Just when I thought I had enough of the mother's worst nightmare, our J died. Do you believe in angels? If not, consider this brief encounter described above that we had. God once again showed His presence in our lives. We were grateful. We continued our gratitude and living the life we believe God wants us to live.

My faith, as I continuously say, is what carries me through. I know I have to please God and show Him I know that He is with me, trust in His presence in my life. I need to show others He is there carrying me through.

Chapter 19

WE ARE NEVER ALONE

God puts people in our lives for profound reasons. Some come and go, and that is okay, because once the purpose of the relationship is fulfilled, we carry on. So how does this play out?

Some people may be those who you casually know who then become a significant part of your life. There are others who may be complete strangers prior to your encounter of meeting and "needing" them. Some can be family members who play a new role in your life. Whatever or whoever it is, recognize the significance of them in your life, at any given time.

One such person was originally someone I knew through a friend, with whom I'd never had any personal reactions to note. This acquaintance was the mother of friends of J's and Alyssa's. This particular friend lost a son four years before we lost J, and he was also at the age of seventeen. This young boy was battling cancer. Sadly after a long, courageous battle with the disease, he passed away. Of particular note is that this happened the day after our Lauren was in that "near fatal" car accident described above. Needless to say, it was hard time for all.

Remember, I talk about no such thing as coincidences. The similarities in timelines with this family are uncanny. When this young boy found out that his cancer returned after a long period of remission, the date was November 15. This date of course is the date that our J went on to eternal life. This is such a point of wonder about how God orchestrates the fabric of our lives and "weaves" us together. That tapestry we can't see until we are in Heaven!

Years later, when we did lose J, knowing the pain and agony of losing a young son who was the same age as we lost our J, this family immediately came to our side to help us through this. The power of their coping and their support to all of us has been immeasurable with our ability to move on. Knowing someone as well as we know this family that we identify with in so many ways provides us the courage and strength that we can do this too. They are always checking in with us. They are affirming our fears, sadness and general feelings of the journey ahead.

I remember our J talking to me about this boy's death and wondering then why God takes such good kids. Can you imagine J asking this and four years later, at the same age, he is with his friend in heaven? J and this young man shared many of the same character traits. It makes you really contemplate life.

Knowing we are far from alone carrying this lifelong struggle, our dear neighbors who lost their only son at age nineteen also provided tremendous support to us. We see how strong they are and it gives us hope and strength that we can do the same. Although we would have never wanted to share this type of life challenge with anyone we know, we feel fortunate to have them for our emotional support and walking this journey with us knowing our "shattered heart" all too well.

We have become closer friends with these families, which is one of the blessings of such a loss. God allows evil for the greater good right? Well, we are hoping that we continue to see the blessings knowing we can't change the fact that J was taken from us. We have many people who chose to join us on our journey. We are very fortunate!

So many strangers have reached out as well. One person has a relative that is a professional colleague of mine. This woman lost her daughter July 2009, just before Jonathan in November. This mother called me and came over with some loving tips on how to travel this road. Being the deaths were so close together, both sudden, both teens and still quite raw, we tended to hold up each other in different ways.

Another woman, whom I never met, anonymously sent me a beautiful sterling silver heart with Jonathan's name on it. She saw the death on the news and in the papers so she wanted to reach out. What a thoughtful gift. What a beautiful, kind gesture. I wear it often. I wonder who she was, no return address, no name, just a beautiful compassionate message. Another one of those "angels" on earth I guess.

Although I am big on seeking whatever help one needs to cope, I mentioned often my approach is to write, read, pray, and reflect. I tend to heal best when I have someone I know to talk to, someone that fully understands me, preferably someone that knows my pain. I have that in these mothers as well as my own mother. How fortunate to have had her with me to help me through this. Mom just left this earth a few months ago in early 2019. There were so many times I felt worse for her because she has the pain of watching me suffer and the direct loss of her dear grandson. Her age at the time of J's death was 86, this shouldn't happen, we know that, and she shouldn't be burying a young person, but God has different plans for us and we have to learn to deal with it. Until the day she died, she never accepted God's choice of taking J so young despite her having lost a baby 60 years prior and then another son, just two years before she passed away. The age of seventeen struck her as "unfair, wrong, his life was just beginning." More often than not I was in a role to console my aging mom. Having such a role makes me seek to be strong for her and others. Being focused outside of yourself helps to see how to be there for others. To stay focused on our own sadness can be a dark place if we stay too long.

Then there are those who just can't come to grips with the pain and suffering and choose to move away from it. This was hard to reconcile. Those people, otherwise close to us, who now couldn't seem to be around us. It hurt a lot. But again, I tend to assume positive intent of others. I learned that at times it is hard when family or some friends remain quiet about their grief, staying away from you and not knowing what to do. While you want to appreciate their way of handling it, it can seem cold at times and difficult, but we chalk it up to their way of coping. Staying away keeps the pain at bay and maybe that's what they need to move on. I would highly recommend moving away from your own feelings and be sure to share your love and kindness with those suffering most. Keeping away is further agonizing for grieving families. I am asked to go comfort many grieving parents, moms in particular. Despite how hard it is to relive that pain, it is more important that I provide some strength to the next one in need. I'm just suggesting we all do that for one another!

Then there are those family and friends who share the pain seemingly like we are, they are there for us, they feel our heart and pain. We know how much they loved our J. That is healing more than they realize. We appreciate every card, every call especially on important dates to remember, J's birthday, J's anniversary of his passing. Means far more than words will ever express. Thank you, such people know who they are and the gift of your compassion is healing.

Those who think enough of my son and us to memorialize him are amazing. There is nothing more healing than to know people want to remember J. I already spoke of the many tributes. We are forever grateful for this! It is helping us through more than anyone realizes. When people act with such compassionate and kindness it forms an impression on your heart. We remember each and every gesture and can remember who did each and every beautiful thing.

REFLECTIONS TO J OVER THE YEARS – the journey of coping continues, forever

As I mentioned, reflections, prayer, thoughts, sharing are all part of my daily life. A few things are noteworthy for this book.

During the Lenten season, we reflect on the fact that in order to fulfill our purpose and God's plans for us, we have to prove we can "carry the crosses" that come our way. One night at mass, there was a large picture at the center of the altar of Jesus dragging the cross while crawling on his knees. I have seen this a million times, I'm sure, but this night I locked my eyes on it. It was illustrating exactly how I was feeling. Some days that is exactly how I feel, and at times the "cross" feels too heavy. Over the years, through all of the support and the grace of God, some days that cross feels so much lighter. It is the same cross but I've gotten stronger and can carry it a bit easier now. That will happen to you out there suffering if you allow God and the people sent to you to help you through whatever struggles you have.

There is some sense of joy again more often than not. Sometimes I feel guilty saying this, not sure why but I have that time when I pause and wonder if it is "right" to feel so joyful. There is never a moment that goes by that when I think of my son and that feeling of full contentment because I am so proud of the life he lived. I'm always hoping he hears me through my thoughts and reflective words.

Messages to my son:

One day when I visited Lew Port, I saw the beautiful mural at the school store in your honor...oh how you would love this J! Also some nice pictures from homecoming and powder puff...watch over your class "Big Guy" and send them peace to enjoy the last half of their year together!

J we know you will help us with our struggles and oh... are we struggling buddy...help us understand...you filled every door, I can't turn without missing you...our deep sorrow will somehow, some day fade but memories of you buddy will NOT! We pray for this day that the deep pain fades, even just a little. (Mom)

Hey buddy, well, we continue to gain strength from your dear friends. We see so many of them around and they write nice messages and show kind gestures always. We really know why you loved them all so dearly. Cara made a beautiful memory canvas for us that we love and will cherish always. Thank you for your friends.(Mom)

Here are some reflections from others:

"Jonathan, Thanks for being a great messenger of God; by your very life you showed us God's love and the meaning and message of living, but especially for teaching me to "Live by faith, one day at a time," which I promise to make every effort to live by every day in the hope of truly living it as you did. I can only hope... to be a fraction of the person you were. Thanks for the direction.to be a fraction of the person you were. Thanks for the direction." (J's Uncle Pat)

"Few times in life someone makes such an emotional connection. Jon was the one who taught me that "it was all okay" "It was all good" and he was absolutely correct! I miss you Jon and your contagious smile. I know you are Lew-Port's resident Angel :) God Bless You "(faculty member, Lewiston Porter High School)

"Dearest sweet J-Mill, I have trouble accepting the fact that you're gone so I won't......it'll be like we went for a while without seeing each other. But I could understand......why God would've wanted you close to him....cause you truly were an angel on earth! I love you and I miss you! (teenage male classmate)

"Our Borrowed Angel ♥ We love and miss you"

"i miss you j-mill.. i hope you're watching over us all..cuz we are all looking up to you. i think about you everyday and i want you to know that, i love you very much a long with everyone else.

AB - all i can say is that 'm blessed to have jmill as my guardian angel, i love you♥

Thinking of U Always
Every time you cross my mind, I break out in exclamations of thanks to God.
Philippians 1:3
Jonathan H. Miller - CP
11-15-09
+

AL- thank you J-Mill♥ - (this was a result of a new tragic accident that no one can explain how her car got across the road and how it did so without her being hit. No injuries, immediately those in the car, felt J protected them...she then wrote this on Facebook).

SMO wrote: "A teacher affects eternity; he can never tell where his influence stops. The same is certainly true of Jonathan and his family. Bless you all."

AJ wrote:

"I had to tell you about the encounter I had at work today. I had on my "Jonathan" bracelet today and I cashed out someone at work who had a Lew-Port football hoodie on. We both noticed each other's accessories. The gentlemen proceeded to ask me how I knew Jonathan. He began to chat with me about what a wonderful boy he was and how he always came over to his house to swim. He said his son scored a touchdown at Friday's game and was practicing real hard to make Jon proud. He said his son keeps his picture in the car with him and has one in his wallet. We both started to talk about the lives that Jonathan touched, and I admit we both got a little teary-eyed. When I began to wipe away my tears, this complete stranger pulled me in for a hug, and we both stood there hugging each other because of the wonderful life Jonathan led. I just thought it was so wonderful how two total strangers from different walks in life can come together and have a friendly exchange all because of Jonathan...had to share with you. Love you lots"

These are just a few samples of the writings of so many people over the years. There were hundreds, I read them all, I cherish them all and I save them all. The messages were very similar so I just shared a few.

Chapter 20

BLESSINGS RESULT FROM OUR CHALLENGES

"The thankful heart opens our eyes to a multitude of blessings that continually surrounds us"

– James E. Faust

Most people look at me strange when I begin to speak about the silver linings of tragedy, especially my tragedy. How do we find the blessings after a tragedy? How does any parent find a blessing in the loss of a child? What lessons could we learn from the loss of someone so dear?

My search for these answers began from day one! How could God allow anyone to take on this much pain? Why did he choose us as those who could handle this? Doesn't he know I live for my children and don't want life without them? What is he trying to "tell us"? Every life event has a lesson and if we can learn the good of it all, we have "passed the test."

Again, my approach to handling my struggles is to read, to pray and to talk through my struggles. Sick of hearing that, yet? But really, it just is that simple. I find those who fully know my pain, those who have the wisdom to share and one who will listen above all. I have all of that in my life, and that my friends, is one huge blessing.

Further, I had a life free of tragedy until I was in my mid-forties. Before that, I buried two elderly grandparents, who lived to their mid-90's and had a great, healthy life. Deaths, although sad, were truly expected and good are the memories of long, great lives lived. I had wonderful parents, they too lived long lives, both well into their mid 90's. They were supportive, totally devoted to their children and we had so much love. We had what some call "home court advantage" growing up in a home that met our every need. My foundation was rock solid.

I continued the path that I learned, to have strong faith, to love others, to give much and to work hard. God blessed me with three beautiful, loving children. I did everything I could to ensure that my children will get what they need to live the life God wants them to live. I was far from perfect, but from what we can see at their young adult ages, they received what God wanted them to and are wonderful people.

I figured that working hard at raising good people would result in three more that could positively impact this troubled world. I knew I had three that could do that. So why would God take one away? He knew J had the qualities this world needs. What is He thinking? There is a blessing when God takes your child?

My strong faith tells me yes, there is, and I need to discover just what the blessings are. I spoke a lot about what we learned of who J was to so many. The life he led and the impact he had. So despite his absence here on earth, his life legacy lives on through all he so deeply touched in many ways.

Here we go! I wanted to list the blessings I "found" to date. I am sure over the years I will continue to learn more about why I have this life to live.

Blessing/lesson one: Love one another.

From an early age I learned this very simple ask of us. My mom had a picture made for me with "love one another" on it and my name. To this day I have this hanging in sight. This important goal that I had my whole life I realized J far exceeded. The "goals" we had for him, to be good, to love everyone and to work hard. He aced that. The impact he had living in this way will never die.

J's friends mentioned they are changed for the better because they knew him. They now know the type of character that has impact on others in a manner that is admirable. Many said they will work harder to be like him as a result.

So the lesson, the blessing of knowing the importance of loving all and acting on it accordingly, is so much more important than many things in life.

"Love the person the way they need to be loved, not the way you want to love. It's not about you. Love is selfless, not selfish". Tony Gaskins

Blessing /lesson two, Live by faith, one day at a time!

During a difficult time in my life, J asked Kevin to take him to the local Fatima Shrine, a place he and I often went together as he was growing up. He wanted to buy me something. He found a rock that said "live by faith, one day at a time" and he told Kevin, "that's what I want to buy Mom." Not only did this get me through this brief struggle, but little did I know that it would be the most profound phrase I would need to carry me through my life.

J changed many lives for the better by his words and deeds. This saying became his very own quote. This saying was put on T-shirts worn at the school, a public school, I may add. It is a powerful, lifelong quote that so many use as a memory of J and the strength such a quote provides.

J lived in just this way. To know J was to know that he lived one day at a time. His heart was light. He stressed very little. He had the faith we all need to have. As he would always say, "relax, everything will be all right," and he showed us how to do that. Through his death, we realized he mastered that. Although we hear it all the time and we think we get it, I really didn't until I felt the pain of a day living without J. *Now I truly know the value and importance of living by faith, one day at a time.*

Blessing/lesson three – Turn challenges into successes.

Jonathan had many struggles in his life, much of them being academic challenges. However, he rarely saw them as struggles. Life is how we choose to perceive it. Struggles are such only if we see them as such. Happiness is a choice. Rather than losing confidence or feeling shy or withdrawn, he made it a part of him and something that he just had to handle. He received special education assistance occasionally and even though he didn't like the special help he received, he knew it had to be there. He made the best of this situation. He learned to love his special ed teacher more than most and he made the time together fun. Some parents told me that J "glamorized" seeking extra academic help. He just knew he had to do this, so he did it with his light heart, great sense of humor and big, warm smile.

Blessing/lesson four – Live to better the lives of others.

I think throughout this book you have seen just how this played out in different ways simply by J being who he was and how he went about his daily life. Jonathan would stop what he was doing no matter who called him. He was selfless, he showed love, charity and dependability. Many told us of their story related to this trait of his. Whether it was a young female friend afraid on a date who called him at late hours to pick her up or his grandma calling him if only to pick up bananas for her, whoever it was, regardless of how seemingly unimportant the request may be, such people benefitted from calling J always.

"Society says, look out for yourself, but God says, look out for others and I will look out for you" author unknown.

Blessing/lesson five – Seek to understand others.

J never judged others. He had friends from all walks of life. His funeral was a clear example of that. I saw people I never saw before. The different groups of kids he was part of. J didn't have any one group that he fully identified with. J was friends with all. He saw each person as a friend despite any differences. He saw the good in people that many others couldn't see.

Since J's passing, we have become close to many people as well as developed friendships with those who were friends of J's. Struggles that I personally felt with some people have turned into opportunities for improved relationships. Appreciating differences in others and trying to understand their perspectives is an incredible gift. That is so what he stood for, the power of this energy through his spirit in his death is incredible.

Blessing/lesson six – Forgive, above all. Relationships with others are most important.

J's outlook on life was one that saw very little negativity. It amazed me actually. I would tend to see the faults and he would quickly identify the strengths. Jonathan taught me to be patient, that no one is perfect and that sometimes, working at something too hard at the expense of finding peace is not a good thing. Being that he lived his life focusing on people first and balancing his own needs in order to balance his life , he truly was always happy. I learned, he is right.

No matter how hard you work, nothing is more important than taking the time to focus on people and taking the time to take care of yourself. So wise beyond his years!

Blessing /lesson seven – Focus on the power of positive thinking. Life is what you make of it.

As previously mentioned, the power of positivity and living in such a manner changes everything. At times I would wonder if he would improve enough if he tends to be so positive but I guess I learned exactly how that played out, right?

J would rarely look at a situation as a negative. He had a way of putting a positive spin on every situation. Attitude is the difference between an ordeal and an adventure. J was always on an adventure. He did this well.

Blessing/lesson eight – above all, the biggest blessing was God's gift of his life.

J's death does not define our life. His life does. One day a person asked me, "If you knew you would lose your son at such a young age, would you have had him?" I know this sounds outrageous, but I fully understood why he would ask this, a stranger so pained by our loss. The answer was quickly yes, yes, yes. The life he led sustains me.

Blessing/lesson nine – Believe in miracles

Pennies, orbs, white feathers, all miracles, all divine intervention - all intended to speak to us when we are listening enough to "hear" messages from above. So many don't recognize this ability, and I challenge you to find out the miracles in your life. Live in the moment and you will find significance to things, happenings, people you meet, in ways you never did before.

What an incredible gift this has been. To know that our loved ones are always with us does help in dealing with the profound loss and sadness related.

Blessing/lesson ten – Sharing our love for others and our journey changes lives for the better.

I have previously mentioned how J's life and his passing have made such a difference in the lives of so many others. A significant connection for me was the conversion of three individuals who had no religion and little understanding of prayer and God's role in our lives. These individuals got to know me through J's death and through spending time with them helping them through their challenges, learning that my faith and God's role in my life and how it has sustained me. These individuals wanted what I had. So three of them became Catholics and I was honored to be asked to be their sponsor and godmother. Honestly, I can't think of a better way to help change someone's life. They now have the "tools" I have to face their challenges. There were also others who stated they began renewing their own faith watching our journey. These, my friends, are profound blessings!

There is a silver lining in all of our challenges, and it is our job to find them, grow from them and embrace our journey.

Chapter 21

God, are you really here?

The following reflects, almost verbatim, my conversations with God.

"I said, God I hurt

And God said, I know

I said, I cry a lot

And God said, that's why I gave you tears

I said, Life is so hard

And God said, That's why I gave you loved ones

I said, But my loved one died!

And God said, So did mine

I said, it's such a great loss

And God said, I saw mine nailed to the cross

I said, But your loved one lives

And God said, So does yours!

I said, where is he now?

And God said, My Son is by My side and your son is in My arms! (author unknown)

Through all of this, it is clear to me that life is a mystery, it is uncertain, it is a challenge, it is the test of who we are and what we are made of. God then decides how well we did in the end, where we all really want to be. If life were easy, we wouldn't be seeking the beauty and peace of heaven. So God makes sure we are not complacent while on this earth.

I would be lying if I told anyone that I didn't ask this very question – at least a few times.

Why do bad things happen to good people?

Bad things do happen to good people, why wouldn't they? God shows no favorites. The most profound explanation I have heard of this concept in a while was found in the book "The Shack" by Wm Young. The analogy that was used in this book that made this concept clear was a scene where a suffering man asked God why he lets bad things happen to good people – bad people should suffer. God replied in this book, "Let me ask you to give me one of your children to suffer, who would you give?" The suffering man became angry and said that he wouldn't be able to give any of them, and God replied, "Then why would I impose suffering on any of my children?" All of us being His children, we know that He loves us the same.

So what is God's role in our lives? When we pray, what should we pray for? Does God stop illness or injury?

God's role has become clearer and clearer to me. It is also very simple. God is there to carry us, to provide us strength, to give us peace and to guide us to live as He desires. Beyond that, free will makes this very muddy. This life is not meant to be easy or pleasant all of the time. Actually we are in a trial throughout our entire life. It is how we handle our struggles that will matter to God. We will all have them. It is free will that explains why God doesn't stop tragedy or illness all of the time. If He feels a person has not completed his or her mission, then a "miracle" may occur. That's the only time from what I have come to believe that God intervenes. Further, that person whom He allows to enter eternal life is one who can help Him guide mortal man in a more effective manner through his or her death. We see such divine interactions often enough to understand this concept.

Upon getting the news of my son's death, there were days, many of them, I just wasn't sure why God allowed us this much suffering. We try very hard to live a good life and so I felt at some level we were being punished. I sought out why and realized after much reflection and understanding and accepting of God's role, that it has nothing to do with us or what we do or did, but rather, it was time for our dear son to go to heaven as his mission was clearly completed. He changed countless lives. He lived the life God wanted him to live. It was time to relieve him of the struggles on earth and come to eternal life with all good and happiness forever.

It took at least a month for me to completely accept God's decision to take my dear son. My heart was so heavy, there were a few mornings when I asked God not to allow me to awaken, since I cannot carry it. It felt as though someone was sitting on my chest. Every day. But I awoke, I showered, I got dressed, I put my makeup on and took it moment by moment since twenty-four hours was far too long to think I could make it through. One day at a time became more of my approach after three months after J's death. Before that, I didn't think in days – it was minutes or hours. By the grace of God, I was functioning, and quite well, despite this extreme life challenge and heartache.

People ask me daily how I do it, like I've said before. There is only one answer. I do it through the grace of my God and my son's spirit. There is no other way. I wouldn't be able to breathe if I didn't have the faith that I do.

Chapter 22

GRIEVING IS A PROCESS –"Live by faith one day at a time"! One hour at a time! Whatever works.

The thing about grieving is that there is no right or wrong way to do so. There is no defined timeline to get through grief. There is no proper order of grieving. There is no comparing one another's grief. Grief is a personal journey. That being said, there are some things that I have found to be valuable.

THE FIVE PHASES OF GRIEF

SHOCK, AWARENESS OF LOSS, WITHDRAWAL, HEALING & RENEWAL

At this stage in my grieving I have visited some, if not all of these, more than once. Grieving is a process. Grieving lasts a lifetime, especially in the loss of a child. Having lost others close to me at older ages, I can honestly say, there is a time grief ends knowing the long, good life well lived. The loss of Jonathan is a totally different grief process.

As previously mentioned, the first week after J's sudden passing, the pain was such that it was physical as much as emotional. It feels as if your heart is literally being sliced and diced. There is immediate fear, insecurity, and feelings of extreme uncertainty in this world that used to be so comforting. Panic sets in. Everything seems out of your control. Fear of losing everyone else comes into your thoughts in a huge way. Extreme loneliness seeps in, despite those around you. At times, a feeling of not being able to breathe, extreme heaviness and pain in the chest becomes overwhelming. A feeling that you are dying and not really caring if you did!

When you are a problem solver by nature and one who can orchestrate and organize life quite well, something like this can make you quickly realize how little control you actually have in life. This journey took us to a place that had no "fix," no ending. We couldn't keep others from the pain this caused, the fear and angst instilled in our daughters who at such a young age had to endure such a loss. I couldn't protect anyone from harm. Being where I am now in this journey, my mantra is, we have little control on what happens to us, but we have total control on how we react to the situation. This gave me back the control I needed. It was up to me to make good of this journey, and finding ways to do so is my constant focus.

Families that openly grieve, share their feelings and thoughts, admit their pain and negative feelings tend to have positive impact on themselves and others. Shutting others out isn't necessarily helpful to the process. You need each other to lean on. You have to be ready to face your pain.

I have found that grief causes tension. There are tensions and irritability that were not as present prior to this grief. There is often unnecessary bickering and disconnect that makes it uncomfortable at times. There is a feeling that when one wants to talk about J, someone else may not, making it difficult for both or all parties involved.

When we feel the pain of others who are trying to determine the best way to talk about J with us, we have learned that it is up to us to take the edge off for them. If they don't know what to say, we try to direct the discussion so they can become comfortable sharing. We have to let them know it is okay, and somehow we will be okay. It is also important that others know how we appreciate their support and how that helps us. After all, this could happen to anyone and people feel vulnerable. I try to tell people that when they speak from a place of love and compassion, it is unlikely their message won't be well received.

A GRIEVING DAD

Kevin added from his journal of healing written in Summer 2010

"This is a father's view of how I am coping with the loss of my son. Nov 15, 2009 changed my life forever. A day I will never forget, not because I want to but because I wish that day could be wiped off the calendar. This is the hardest thing a parent will ever go through. Many people compare this to the loss of a parent, in my opinion it is not even close. To watch your child grow for seventeen years, watch his successes and failures, watch him mature into a fine young man that helps others and give back to society. Then have all that wiped out is just unbearable. I used to wonder, watching the news about a child that died and how those parents would have to deal with it, now I know. Dealing with it may not even be the appropriate words. You are getting out of bed, going to work, having free time with other family members. But, are you really dealing with it? The few things that have helped is talking with others that have gone through this or more appropriately, going through this as you never really get over it. Seeing my son's friends whether it is at a store, on the golf course or even when they stop by the house is very difficult. As hard as it is, I hope that never ends. Seeing Jonathan's friends and finding out how well they are doing in school or in their careers makes me happy to see. I remember the first time I went to play golf after Jonathan passed away. I was just about to finish the first hole when I saw two of his friends Brandon and Matt coming off the sixth green. When we locked eyes it was like no one needed to say a word. We just walked toward each other and gave a great big hug. Sometimes words can't express the feelings a hug can. Hearing stories about Jonathan and how he influenced other's lives before he passed and how he is still influencing lives to this day, make me so proud of him. Jonathan was the type of son who was very convincing when he wanted to do something. I often joke how he would ask to do something that we weren't convinced made sense at the time. Before Jeannine and I knew it he was on his way out the door to do it and I was sticking a twenty-dollar bill in his back pocket. That's how convincing he could be. Jonathan never let us down. I think that is why we seldom questioned him about what was going on.

There were several nights he would come into our room at 1:00 or 1:30am. And say he would be right back. Jeannine and I would look at each other then, Jeannine would say "let us know when you get back." Sometime later, even a few times after he passed, we would find out he was going out to pick up a friend whose date was drunk or something and they knew they could count on Jonathan. These were little things that mean so much. Even the number of people that showed up for his wake and ultimately his funeral, told us so much about Jonathan as a person, friend, teammate.

Talking with the family, Jeannine and the girls, helps a lot as well. I say talking but I really mean listening because many times it is too hard to talk. I start talking and only get a couple words out before I completely lose it. Jonathan is inside my thoughts every minute of every day. As much as you may love someone while they are alive you have no idea how much more you love them when they are not there.

Several years before Jonathan passed away he wanted me to take him to The Fatima Shine near our house to look for a mother's day present for his mom. This is a place Jeannine used to go to each week to light a candle and just pray. After looking at several items he decided on a rock that read "Live by faith one day at a time." I can't tell you how important that saying and rock means to her. I think sometimes that one day at a time is too long. One minute at a time seems more like it. We both find ourselves inspired by that rock. Many times people will ask me how we are coping with his loss and my reply is "Faith, Family and Friends."

Jonathan was a hard worker, lots of friends, but at the same time there were many people that Jonathan didn't know but would bump into during his day. They have told us many times how that little bump meant so much to that person. Thinking how I will never see Jonathan, in this life, again makes it so hard. He was my little buddy, my golf partner, my sport enthusiast, someone to watch games with.

Over time I hope to organize my thoughts, right now everything is just so scrambled. I take each day as it comes. Deal with what is in front of me. Many people say you shouldn't keep this type of issue bottled up inside of you. The problem is even talking about it the bottle doesn't empty out it just keeps filling up. You wonder how big the bottle can get.

Sometimes it is hard to go out and see people, you know they are moving on with their lives and you are not sure how you will be able to as well. Even the smile you put on the outside doesn't reflect what is going on inside. It is good to be out. I am not the type of person to stay isolated.

Sometimes when I would see a person out and our paths cross you could see it in their eyes how vulnerable they felt. If losing a son can happen to someone they know it can happen to anyone. One father told me that he just wanted to drive to his daughter's school that day and give his daughter a big hug even though she was going to be driving home the next day. This father just wanted the assurance that she was going to be there. Many times I had to diffuse the situation by going up to them and just say "good to see you," try to put that person at ease.

The night of the accident the police wouldn't let us get close to the scene when all I wanted to do was run down there and hug and kiss him and tell him for the millionth time how much I love him and how proud I am of him. Having never seen him on that last night still pains me. One night my wife and I were talking about Jonathan and how we feel we have no regrets from the standpoint of telling him how much we love him. I imagine some parents wish they would have said it more but we were comfortable how we always told him that. We say it many times to his sisters as well. The kids used to call me corny because I would tell them how they all had unlimited potential. Little did we know Jonathan was reaching his unlimited potential beyond all belief. When he came into our room at night to say good night I would always say

———

"love you bud." Sometimes he would even give you one of his famous head butt kisses, where he would just lean his head down into you. You knew what he meant but I would just kiss him on the top of the head or the side. I knew it was his way of kissing me.

Every day I would get up, get ready for work, smile at people I passed though out the day and wonder how am I going to get through this day. I never saw myself as a selfish person but I miss him so much I just want him back. There were many times when I thought God was the selfish one. God knows how much good Jonathan was doing on earth with his friends at school, teammates, family members and even people he didn't know and yet God wanted him for himself. I know that's not the right way to think, but that's how I feel. People always say that God takes you when your mission on earth is accomplished, Well Jonathan mission well done. If God knows the hole he left in our hearts he may have thought twice. Some people say the hole in our hearts is the piece that Jonathan took with him. I know with all the pieces of hearts from his mother, sisters, grandparents, aunts, uncles, cousins, friends I know now why he has such a big heart.

Many times throughout the day, when I go to sleep at night, wake up in the morning I see his face. I would see that big smile he always had on his face. I think about all the good things he did for people, the stories his friends would tell about him and how Jonathan changed or influenced their lives. Just then a simple smile would come over me, knowing that Jonathan was my son.

You wonder how much suffering a person can take. I hope my other two children Lauren and Alyssa know that even though we talk about Jonathan a lot, that it is not meant to take away from them, they are two beautiful people on their own. We love our girls just as much as we love Jonathan and are as proud of them.

For a while I was the golf coach at a local university. This meant that I had to travel during the spring and fall months. I knew that when I did I could always count on Jonathan to be there for Jeannine and the girls. During those times Jonathan was the man of the house. He knew to make sure the doors were locked at night and help Jeannine and the girls with whatever he could to make it easier on them when I was gone. My first trip in the spring of 2010 was very difficult for me knowing Jonathan wasn't there. I knew he was there in his own way, but of course, not the same.

The second hardest day of my life

Jeannine and the girls were talking about putting a cross on the tree that stopped Jonathan's car that awful night in November. This was the tree where everyone gathered to tell stories and pray following Jonathan's passing. Not sure why, but when a young person dies there always seems to be a tree involved. Maybe this is God's way of giving people a place or location to go back to or drive past that helps keep that person's memory alive. I know I will never forget, but even so, when I drive past I always give a quick glance and say I love you dude. We all know that Jonathan died before he hit the tree but yet that has become the place where we will hang a wreath or flowers to let him and others know we will never forget.

I never thought in a million years making a cross in my garage was something I would ever do. So many times I would pass a cross on the side of the road and think I wonder what happened, how are the parents and other relatives doing? How are they handling this loss? I don't remember if I told anyone I was going to build a cross for his tree but one morning after gathering some material and paint I went out to the garage to do just that. I didn't have any appointments that day until the afternoon so thought I would get started. I don't know if I was trying to kid myself into the idea that it was just a project that I had to get done or what but I can tell you it only took a few seconds before I completely lost it.

The pain I felt in my gut was beyond anything you could imagine. I had to stop several times because I couldn't see with the tears were flowing so fast. Building this cross was becoming an impossible task. After actually getting the cross put together I wanted to put his nickname on it. All of Jonathan's friends called him J-Mill, a name that still sticks today. I also added his football number, 76. The high school Jonathan went to retired his football jersey. Funny how things turn out because years ago I used to tell the kids the best exercise was to reach down and pick someone up. This was something I had heard myself years earlier and such a catchy phrase. I am glad Jonathan took this to heart and to its true meaning.

After the cross was finished, paint and all, I took it to the tree to hang. I left the tree that day a complete and total mess. I wasn't sure I wanted to have an afternoon of work appointments but knew I had to. After leaving the house that afternoon I stopped at a convenience store that at the time I had only been to a couple times. I purchased a bottle of water and a newspaper. I was walking away from the counter when the clerk said "Excuse me" to get my attention. When I turned around she said "Can I just tell you how nice you look today?" The clerk was a young girl probably about twenty years old. This young lady had no reason to say that to a man of my age. I couldn't help but wonder if God put this person in my life, at that time, in order to pick me up. I walked out of the store feeling a little better that day.

The cross I hope will last forever so people will always remember Jonathan. One of a parent's worst nightmares is that people will forget. Hopefully this will be just one reminder of what a great son, brother, friend we all lost that day.

The grief of Kevin, as J's dad, is typical of how he rolls with all of life's struggles, with tremendous composure and grace. Kevin was always an active part of every aspect of raising our children. Nothing was beneath him and he loved every bit of their lives. As one who protects us, he felt helpless.

We need to realize that we cannot remove grief but we need to experience it and allow the feelings that come with it. Allowing yourself to cry is very important. Allowing yourself to say "no" to events, things you really don't feel you are strong enough to handle for whatever reason, is very important. Give yourself space. Don't take on new things that will add to your tensions, Kevin says.

A GRIEVING MOM

J's death – the strength to carry on…something I would have told anyone was impossible for me. My children are everything to me – my purpose, my reason for living and the joys of my life. How could I do without any one of them? How will I be able to do this?

It seems that mothers are conditioned differently than men, and early on, we are "allowed" to show our feelings and openly cry. We can express our fears openly, and this is something we know from when we are little girls, and as young girls we are oriented to be nurturers and to care for others, especially family. As we grow older and then marry, we have visions of our role as a mother. For me, the minute I became a mother, I expected that I could create a secure place for my family and everything revolved around tending to the needs of our children. It was my pleasure to do so.

Four days before my thirtieth birthday I received yet another of God's greatest gifts, my third child, my first and only son. The baby of our family was born. No longer did I ever feel another birthday gift was necessary. I received the greatest gift – another child. J was that child. He was healthy, fun-loving, and "all boy." We all enjoyed the differences that a boy brings to the household. We cherished every day of his life.

J's death has brought many struggles. The constant reminder of his absence around the house and spending time with me is at times unbearable. Missing out on the milestones, especially in his senior year in high school. Not being able to see his senior year through after all of his hard work, especially since this would have been a fun year with some pressure off. He had just received his acceptance to college.

Why would God allow such suffering?

What have we done to deserve this much pain and sorrow for the rest of our lives? Getting angry with God is not the prominent feeling, but when it comes on, it comes on hard. The guilt of being angry with God exists as well. But I do realize God understands my heart and forgives. God is loving and forgiving. God is NOT a punishing God.

"Bad things happen to good people" all of the time. Accidents and imperfections in our physical makeup happen that cause our bodies to stop functioning, as that seems to be what happened to our J. Maybe it was a heart ailment that was undetectable or perhaps a head injury, slow bleed from football. We will never know, as an autopsy wasn't possible due to the damage of hitting the tree as his SUV drove into it after he had died while driving. A seemingly perfectly healthy young man dropped dead with no warning.

I am at peace that although it was a short life, it was a full life that will live on forever through the impact he had on so many lives.

No one is spared the struggles in life. Happiness often comes slowly so we must work at it and be patient with ourselves, but we have to know that we become stronger, learning something new as a result of each and every challenge despite its magnitude!

Others find some of my approaches have been helpful, so I want to share them with you:

- Finding your NEW NORMAL is the challenge. Many of us don't like change of the smallest types, and this type of "change" is beyond comprehension. Take it hour by hour at first, day by day afterward. Recognize you will not change what has happened, you only have control on how you will handle it!

- Insecurity is a common reaction at first. Face your fears and discomfort head on. Show yourself you can "still do it." Each success, as small as it may be, builds your stamina.

- Get out and about as early as possible after the death. Remove yourself from the oppression that sadness keeps you in. Find some places that bring you peace and visit them.

- Focus on the blessings and positives in your life. REMEMBER your loved one is now safe and happy forever, so it is up to you to ensure that those around you as well as yourself will make the best of the life you still have to live.

- Quiet time and alone time is important.

- I went away to remove myself from the routine for a while. I find that being alone can begin to allow you to find yourself once again. Being a mother, you define yourself as that and spend little time on who you really are as a person, so once something like this happens, you have to find your "happy place"…listening to music of when I was young has helped, experiencing places I used to be when I was young and carefree…rebuilding my crumbled foundation is what was important. I would recommend everyone consider this.

- I cry, okay, sob, when I need to.

- I talk about J when I need and want to. I speak of him as recognition of his life.

- I reach out to others when I need to or when I'm called to, which was a regular part of my life for years.

- I say what I feel more than I ever did.

- I express my love for others openly verbally and through actions more often.

- I do not worry about anything. That's right – nothing. This clearly taught me that nothing changes by worrying, so it is useless energy and you lose the value of the moments as a result.

- I surrender that God is totally in control and how freeing that is.

- I now actually really do live one day at a time.

- I now tend to my needs as often as possible.

- I find time to cry alone to avoid bringing others down.

- I seek out people who provide the support I need.

- I recognize to not spend time planning outcomes, as it won't really change them.

- I sleep as much as I need to since grief simply wears you out!

- I know that God provides the strength for us to carry on and obtain the peace we need.

The key is that we all have to give each other space, avoid judgment, and please, unless you have had a loss that is exactly the same as the person you are supporting, there is NO WAY you know what they are feeling, so please refrain from using that phrase "I know how you feel". Just be there, just hug them, and just let them know they are as important as ever to you.

I also learned that those who are in Heaven have a way of knowing who needs them most at any given time. They will "show" to those that they feel they need to in the time that is appropriate. Remember the section on "messages from heaven"? I don't long for J to come to me because if I need it, he will, and God knows that. But I do wish I could remember his voice, and I certainly remember his comments, his laughter and his warmth – but just to hear his voice again.

Having two grown adult daughters at the time of J's death has made this more bearable. They are mature beyond their years. They have strong faith, and they have wisdom and are bright so it makes them extremely supportive to me. I have found it important to allow them to share as they feel they want to. The challenge to me is that I don't talk about J too much and that I assure my girls that their being with me is my strength to move through this. I love them all the same. J is happy now in Heaven, so we needed to figure out how to create our "new normal" and new family dynamics without pushing our loss away. Balancing the loss and missing of J is our forever challenge.

GRIEVING TOGETHER

So often we hear of marriages failing after the death of a child. I fully understand how this could happen. We are far from thinking clearly. We go through a focus of just our own pain not able to see others. We don't care much about other things in life when we are deep in grief so we miss opportunities to be there for others at times.

For those couples who suffer to the point of resulting in a marriage breakup, I often wonder if maybe there were already significant issues related to the relationship. If so, this certainly would be a tipping scale to ending the marriage. Who has any energy to deal with other things when something like this hits you?

So often we displace our angst and blame whoever is closest to us. "We tend hurt the ones we love."

In any case, I want to provide hope for those who are struggling in their relationship while on this journey and maybe what helped us will ring true for you.

First thought is that no one loves the same person as much as you both do. That is a deep connection. You both created this beautiful life together. The shared love of a child is profound to me.

Second, we recognize the differences in how we grieve and supported that. Checking in periodically to be sure we were balancing one another. As Kevin indicated, he liked when I talked about J but he found it difficult to do so himself without completely falling apart. Kevin was quiet about it, so I had to use a lot of other clues to be sure he was all right beyond his words. Kev, much like J, has the gift of positive thinking.

Hold one another closer, tighter. Move away from yourself and focus on the needs of your grieving partner. This is healing in many ways. When we seek to comfort others, such comfort is returned as doing good for others, and it nurtures the soul.

Be open and honest about feelings and share them with one another. Believe me, Kev was a punching bag on some days where my feelings got away from me, but as he remained peaceful, I would find comfort. I would hope I did the same.

Today we can say we are stronger as a couple. I know I cherish him more than I ever did and I didn't think that was possible. Through trials like this, you see other things in people you never had the mindfulness to see.

This type of trial that rips you to shreds makes you or breaks you. God's healing hands carries us both to today, and we are feeling grateful to have one another to hold on to. I can't think of anyone else that I would want to comfort me than a person who is grieving the same profound loss of our child.

My husband and I shared our lives together for so many years, so many ups and downs and we held each other through it all. When in my darkest moments, who else knows how to heal my heart better?

Chapter 23

WHAT I HAVE LEARNED ABOUT DEATH

"Astonishingly enough, life does not end with death. We live forever. In the light of that truth, all other things, including the most severe trials of life, pale by comparison. But upon that last breath, we'll rise out of our bodies, look down upon what were our physical "vehicles" and either linger for a while (perhaps to assist loved ones in their grief)_ or go immediately into a Light that will shortly and wondrously be described to you" (Michael H. Brown, uncle of Jonathan, my brother, author of The Other Side)

I now view death so differently than I once did. We tend to view death as a sad, tragic occurrence. Why do we view being born to eternal life as a tragedy? The reason we do so is because of how we feel with the loss of someone we love. The selfish response that we all tend to have is because we will miss this person. The tragedy is that we continue to struggle on earth, NOT the death. Death is a reward, recognition for a job well done, mission accomplished! I no longer fear death and I know that my son is at peace and will never struggle, be sick or have sorrow – ever. There is a very strong sense of peace knowing that. I never have to worry about him not being happy and having a successful life. He had a more successful life than many who live to be ninety years old!

It took my son's death for me to reflect on death, God's role, my strength, my faith and my ability to adapt. What I have learned is that God is so present in our lives. God is providing me so much strength and my faith allows me to know that I will see J again and that he is in a better place. I truly believe he is.

To take quotes from J's eulogy written by his Uncle Mike Brown:

"He is in a place of radiance beyond the brightness of earth/in a place of colors beyond earthly colors, in a state where he can see us and be with us especially when we pray

Jonathan is now waiting for the day when we can join him/waiting with that big strong softness/with his easy way/ in that light/ and it is in that light that we'll see him again

The next time we encounter Jonathan he will be in the place of luminosity, beyond this valley of rain and tears where realities unfold unto eternities

Life is tough, life can be gruesome, life can be a horror, as we have seen, but it all pales beside the light that comes after. In that light, the light Jonathan now wears, no test is too great

This is not a tragedy more than it is a success story, a day for sorrow, yes, excruciating, but a day of congratulations to him

God is love and love is the light of life, here and hereafter. Jonathan Harold had that.

What remain as mysteries are meant to remain mysteries and what are tragedies to us are graduations to the Lord

Jonathan, you know what the earth is all about now, what the stars are all about and what lies beyond

We know you will help us in our struggles, the blindness of earth

We know you will help us understand

We will sense your presence in the rays of sun and even when there are clouds

In the end tragedy will be the wrong way of calling this; it was a completion

For now we'll hear your voice in the whisper of the wind and in the nudges of intuition, in "coincidence" in the resonance of God, in the chimes of Heaven at the periphery of consciousness, in the recesses of dreams

There is no lights out, no fade to black

God needs J's brightness back and one day you'll share it again in a place of that eye has not seen

When we look at the sky and a star twinkles brightly, we'll think of you Jonathan

Your smile defeated darkness

Your smile will always live"

Michael H. Brown (Author, journalist, my brother, and uncle of Jonathan)

Do you believe this?

I would like to challenge all to reflect on Mike's eulogy comments, to read up on those death experiences that would support this view of death. When we read books about those that have died and returned to earth, the common theme is that they did not want to return. What they experienced in their death, though brief, providing them with the peace and serenity that we hope Heaven provides. A good life lived deserves a reward and that is death and heaven.

I believe the love that my son had for us lives within us. We feel his presence in so many ways. We have experienced those "coincidences" or "messages and miracles" that assured us when we were unsure.

"Persistence is a deeper walk of faith. When we maintain faith, persist beyond persistence and hope beyond hope, the God of miracles is near. The smaller we are, the larger He is. Heaven hears our pleas and is with us every inch of the way. It doesn't seem like it at times…but the graces are there if we look for them" (Michael H. Brown, author of God of Miracles)

Understanding God in our life is tricky at times. I think we give Him credit and blame Him too often. I really think that we are guided by God, and our experiences and humanely desires move us to our decisions. Most of the time, we are fine, but some of our decisions become learning experiences because maybe they didn't turn out so good. Our imperfections inevitably cause us some choices and experiences that are not the best route to go.

I have found that if we "listen" carefully to God, we will be in alignment and most things will go very well for us. What we want is not necessarily what is best for us. Therefore, we must remain open and flexible, changing our path when barriers keep arising. Such barriers, I feel, are God's messages to change our path.

God answers every prayer, and some answers are not what we had hoped.

"The Lord stretches us and forges us and folds us. He holds us like metal over a flame. He presses us, and applies a polish that we might be a reflection of Him". "You've heard the analogy of how gold is purified by fire. So it is with us. He molds us through trials, and once we accept that we transcend it. With each little test, we gain grace, and grace works the wonders."(Michael H. Brown)

What I learned from traditional religion and what I now believe after years of life experiences and striving to understand God is that God is love. Period. He is all good. He is there for us to lean on, to trust in, to give us strength. Again, God is NOT a punishing God. From the book "The Shack" (Wm Young) the role of God became extremely clear. In this book, the role of God was one that was non- judgmental, non –hierarchical and neutral in power. God doesn't see us as different, good or bad. We are loved the same. We are treated the same. He provides us all the same support. The "needlepoint" that God has created as the way He wants things to be, is scrambled by our choices, free will, and accidents or illness that may result. If you look at the back of a needlepoint you see threads that are knotted and crossed, that is reality of life, the perfect picture on the other side is not possible with free will. The tapestry of life.

From the book and movie "Lovely Bones" (by Alice Sebold) Heaven and the interaction of those who have left this earth and those of us left on earth to cope. The young brother who came in to tell his dad that Susie (his sister who had been murdered) came to him, hugged him, the young boy says "she listens to us." The father mentioned that she came to him as well, through "seeing" her one evening while thinking about her looking into a burning candle, through a window and the reflection was another candle that was blowing differently. That clearly wasn't simply a reflection, as we would have imagined it to be. The person Susie met in Heaven who took her under her wing when she first arrived explaining what Heaven was like encouraging her to let go of earth and embrace her new place, where she can be carefree and be the person she wants to be without hesitation. This to me showed that at one point, she was on her journey through Heaven, a "level" of Heaven but not quite "there yet." This same comment was made to Jonathan's friend, Jeff, in a visionary dream if you recall earlier in the book. When Jeff asked "are you in Heaven yet" when J came to him in the dream, J stated "not yet." There are some things that those who have left us, still have to do, unfinished "business" that God allows before they reach their "graduation," the place we all long to be when we leave this earth - the entrance through the golden gates.

Letting our loved ones go

In one scene in Lovely Bones, Susie's mother finally got up the strength to go into Susie's room. Susie, with her commentary from Heaven in the movie, stated that her mom was finally accepting that Susie was in Heaven and allowed Susie to move through. For me, knowing J was at peace and with God came very early. This allowed me the peace to know, my dear son was safe and with God in a place that we all long to be. Free of earthly troubles, stresses, challenges and sadness. He loved his life and lived it well. Now he is in eternal life, where he will be happy and healthy forever and ever. There are ways that those that have left us let us know they are "okay." J has sent this message to many of his cousins and his sister through visionary dreams.

Those we love who have left us want us to learn how to cope and move on. We have to honor them and do just that. As hard as it is, we have to learn that we have work to do, God has a plan for us and we need to ensure we can fulfill it.

We will be with him once again, and while we will try to enjoy the good in our lives right now, we will look forward to that day we are altogether once again for all eternity!

Chapter 24

God's plan for my life

Reflection of my life mission

No stranger to difficulty, no different than most, I have found that rebounding from each and every trial has made me stronger, wiser and more compassionate. You never can stop improving on any of these traits.

There is so much that I don't understand. My only option is to put my trust in God. I have found extraordinary strength. I have found extraordinary peace. I have found the ability to have joy and laughter back into my life. I know if you are suffering right now and try some of the things that worked for me, I know you can, too!

Hope

Hope is what gets me through each day. One day I know that when I find my eternal reward, my tears will be wiped away, my questions answered and I will see my J again.

The temporary nature of life is a welcome thought

How does this grab you? Does it sound gloomy?

It isn't that I want to move to eternal life early, but I look forward to a home with perfection and complete contentment. I look forward to seeing my loved ones once again, whom God called before me. Losing a child has brought me with a feeling of Heaven that I never had the mind to consider. It has made death a positive experience. I feel my son's peace, and I did so from the first few days he went to eternal life. The visionary dreams have confirmed his contentment. I have never slept better. I have very little stress in my life. I live in the moment. That keeps my foundation steady for the rough roads that life brings on. A life well lived, and he was a parent's dream child! A longer life wouldn't have made his full life better necessarily, it was powerful, and from all accounts provided, he seemed ubiquitous. God presented J everywhere, especially where there were needs.

I work hard to ensure I have a place in Heaven when my mission is complete. I work hard to ensure the legacy of my son lives on. I ensure that I am strong for those looking to me for that comfort, for that ability to live on after the loss of a child. I always felt that I have many eyes on me. I have no choice but to live out the mission God has for me and do it well. My constant prayer is that I do this and do this well.

If going through such a challenge can result in good, in a big way, what am I doing to ensure people see this?

GOD SENDS HIS LOVE THROUGH PEOPLE

This is something we experienced and continue to experience in a tremendous way. Frankly, without such compassionate support provided to us, we would not be moving toward wholeness. Friends have come to us in countless ways to show their love and support. God is with us through this journey in ways that are unexplainable but yet plain to see to me. God has provided us with filling some of the void. Our J could never be replaced, the void never be completely filled, but the void of our hearts are being filled by God, the Holy Spirit and J's spirit, making this journey possible to continue on in a positive way. "*Weeping may last for the night, but there is a song of joy in the morning*" (Joel 2:18-32).

"*Be wise in the way you act toward those who are outside the Christian faith. Make the most of your opportunities. Everything you say should be kind and well thought-out so that you know how to answer everyone*" (Colossians 4:5, 6).

God is providing me the opportunity to share love so that others may learn of His role in finding peace in this difficult journey called life.

Renewal

I find I have been in a state of renewal for some time. This is the tough one since total renewal seems impossible. I do see the changing process, though, and I can laugh and enjoy life. I have changed some of my sobbing into dancing. This is the true outward appearance of God's work and our strong faith.

Over many of my challenges in life, I have learned about the power of perception, how I think and how that will influence my life and how others view me. Coping is a skill that is developed through challenges turned into triumphs. Unfortunately, I have had a bit too much experience in refining this skill, but I can only say that your current challenges, difficulties, sad times will require changing the way you handle and choose to perceive them.

Our minds are powerful tools. We are what we think. You need to be able to determine what God really wants of all of us. That is to be good, positive, loving and kind.

Rebuilding your life is possible, but only with God.

So I have to say that I'm most grateful for the gift of being able to perceive whatever comes my way in a manner that turns me into a stronger version of me. I live in the moment to enjoy each and every encounter of my life. If feeling weak and sad, I pray to find that strength to gain it all back. I seek the lessons in both good and challenging experiences. Personal growth is always important. I shock people when I say I am amply blessed. I get that surprised look. It has been said, "Well, I don't know about blessed," and I reply "yes, blessed." I say this because none of us are spared difficulties in life. The difference is the gift of coping, hope and the blessings that we find when we seek the lesson in the experience.

Each person determines the magnitude of the difficulty. Someone who is devastated over a divorce, for example, may have a worse life and worse reaction than what has happened to us. It's all about how we deal with it – it's that "simple." The difference, my friends, is all about faith, attitude, love and most of all, God's grace. The glass is half full. It just is.

We focus on our blessings rather than our sadness. We all have sadness. If we didn't, we wouldn't know joy. We all have both in our life all the time.

We need to live fully in J's absence.

Don't get me wrong; the fabric of my life has been torn apart. But the good part of this is that we are "stitching" it back together. A huge part of that fabric and the ability to put it back together in a manner that is productive is the spirit of the one we love so dearly and who has left a legacy of pure love, joy and kindness. Our job is to honor this and live this to carry the spirit on!

The impact Jonathan had on so many has made this journey one that is being taken with a large group of people. At times, some feel that others move on and forget about the intense grief of those closest to the loved one lost. In our case this is different. The tributes that are covered in this book identify how this has been made a bit easier. When you have so many people that loved J, learned from him and care about us, this keeps his memory alive, and the healing process moves more forward more peacefully. We are not alone! God has sent His people, to be there with us. He knew we needed this to move toward putting the "fabric" back together.

I never knew sadness until this level of grief struck. Although I would have done well learning this without it, I know that I will offer those I encounter more by living fully on this rocky road.

That's my journey, that's my mission, and that's the only thing that will make this worth going through.

Prayer is powerful, pray often. Pray for strength, for peace, for joy, for direction. It takes patience when going through struggles.

"When you sing to God, when you praise Him, when you worship Him, God gives you peace that you cannot understand" Thelma Wells

Written by a friend to me on Facebook, and similar sentiments sent our way by others as well. "You are an inspiration to so many people you don't even know. God has turned your tragedy into a beautiful testimony of how He can bring us through the toughest of trials. God is faithful."

These types of affirmations tell me that I am on the right "track" to fulfilling my mission in this life.

Chapter 25

WHAT SHOULD FAMILY AND FRIENDS DO FOR GRIEVING PARENTS

Now that I have shared so much about my personal journey of "renewal," I want to share what I've learned in order to help others, since so often people ask what they should do to help others.

Well, we all know how uncomfortable it is when something happens to someone and you just don't know what to do. This is a million dollar question. Do any of us know what to do when something of this magnitude happens? We are all so sad, uncomfortable and worried about making something worse. At times, we react strangely as a result. Remember, you can't make the situation "worse," the situation has defined that. My response to this is go with your heart. Be sensitive to how the family feels once you encounter them. Silence is sometimes the best "comment." A hug is often the best response.

So what can you do to ease the difficulty? Some practical tips!

- Visit, just "be" present.

- Bring meals, preferably a month or so later. We had so much food coming to us that restaurants decided to coordinate with one another or give us a gift card because they realized how much was coming right away. We had meals for months, and that helped, since I didn't feel like cooking for months!

- Shop for the family basic needs; we had no food in the house, and who felt like shopping?

- Offer assistance with household chores.

- Keep in touch with them, often and for the long run.

- Do something special to memorialize the loved one - our biggest fear is people will forget our Jonathan, and that is the biggest fear of losing anyone I believe, but especially a child.

- Do NOT avoid the family. Give a simple hug or hello, or "nice to see you" is all they need.

- Offer to take care of small children if that is the situation for someone you know.

- Pet-sit.

- House-sit.

- Do laundry.

- Mow the grass or rake leaves.

- Send cards or letters that include memories of the deceased child (we had these for years, literally, and what a good feeling it was to receive a random card).

- Assist with thank-you cards after the funeral.

- Invite the family out to dinner, coffee or to your house.

- Offer to go to the cemetery with them.

- Offer cleaning help, especially of the deceased child's room, when the family is ready (this varies tremendously).

- Help sort out the personal belongings of the child.

- Continue phoning and visits long after the death.

- Recognize the need for some grieving to keep visits and going out to short stints, as stamina to visit or be out in public can be a challenge

- Be there and love them.

- Allow the family to talk about their deceased child/sibling/relative. Distractions from such discussions can create tension and frustration since that is all they are thinking about, at least early on in the grieving.

- NEVER offer advice as to how someone should grieve.

- Allow crying, it is medicinal, and do not feel that what you said or did caused it, as the sadness comes from the grief and the tears are healing.

- Suffering of this nature is a journey for a lifetime, and a death of a child is a "life sentence," therefore, keep your support up indefinitely.

- Often a spontaneous visit is more appreciated than a planned visit, as sometimes when someone is stressed and grieving, thinking about "entertaining" adds more stress. If you just stop by and they are up for it, you will determine the length of your stay – read the situation.

Obviously not all of the above things will work for everyone. See what naturally fits your comfort levels, but keep in mind, any good you want to do will be deeply appreciated, even if the family doesn't accept your offers.

Chapter 26

THE OSCILLATING NATURE OF EMOTIONS THROUGH A LIFELONG TRIAL OF THIS NATURE

I believe that God created us to be resilient. We have to believe that we are capable of getting through whatever we encounter. We need to believe in ourselves. This is necessary since there is no getting over the death of a child; there is just getting through it in the most positive way possible. There are many times I feel that I am going to crumble, and I do. I sink to a chair and just sob, from the bottom of my toes, and every ounce of strength that I have goes into getting this deep sadness out. It happens often, and it is necessary to act on it. I will never be okay not having my dear son. I am seeking ways to make my life have purpose and to continue to be a good role model for my daughters and live fully for the joy of their lives. Oh, what joy they bring to me! To show others that God gives us grace to move on.

I do experience joy. I feel happy for others. I am social once again. I love and am nourished by those around us!

Forever Family

Remembering a fine young man. As written by a friend.

November 15, 2010

We reflect and celebrate Jonathan "J. Mill" Miller. We reflect the fine young man who so often touched the lives of others in what he did, and what he valued. In the Catholic faith, the passing of a loved one is celebrated as a rebirth, to be reborn into the Kingdom of Heaven, to that his rebirth is celebrated in one's own way!!

My dear J, You are forever on my mind, in my heart and your spirit works through me each and every day. I'll see you again, I love you forever J.

"LIFE IS GOOD TODAY" (Zac Brown, "Toes")

Jeannine Brown Miller

Photo credit: Scientific Magazine

Acknowledgements

I would like to take the time to note the many people who inspired me to write this book.

First my fellow grieving mothers who, together for each other, provide support, healing and love shared unique to those who share the loss of a child. The Lew Port school community, specifically Jonathan's friends, teachers, and his principal at the time, Paul Casseri. The Lewiston community at large who continue to be supportive, loving, and kind in so many ways. Keep the "messages" coming and share them, as we all know that Heaven speaks to us in many ways. For the many new close friends who came to us through our tough times and remain the best of friends.

To my mother and father who were by my side through it all until their recent passings, encouraging me to, someday, be sure to write a book about my journey of how I was sent to help so many other grieving parents as well as the ways in which I seek peace, hope, and joy despite it all. One of the last conversations I had with my mom prior to her sudden death in January 2019 was related to writing this book. While I hadn't planned to, contemplating her strong desire for me to do so made me stop and review my journal that I had not touched for many years. My mom's words of encouragement to write made me seriously revisit this and I am grateful that I did.

To my brother Michael H. Brown, who is a best-selling author, for his expression of encouragement in the early stages of my writing. Given his extraordinary expertise, without his vote of confidence in the content of this book, I'm not quite sure I would have pursued it.

To my talented niece Elizabeth Katona, who through her expertise, proofed, and edited. And through her input, added to my confidence to seek publication of my journal writings in this manner.

To my sister Maureen Cacace who illustrated the cover using the first feather we ever received as her inspiration.

To my husband Kevin and daughters, Lauren and Alyssa, who are the reason for my living the best life I can and recognizing the joy that remains in this life every single day. They provide me with so much love and laughter, and together we are a strong loving family unit. To my "sons," Jim and Jeff, who now complete our family in a significant, heartwarming way.

Thank you all for your profound love and support of me.

To many friends and acquaintances who are full of love, compassion, and kindness. Thank you for supporting me and expressing to me your perceived strength in me that I haven't been able to see in myself.

Finally, I thank God for always showing me the way, carrying me through the most difficult days, and reminding me of His love and presence in my life every day.